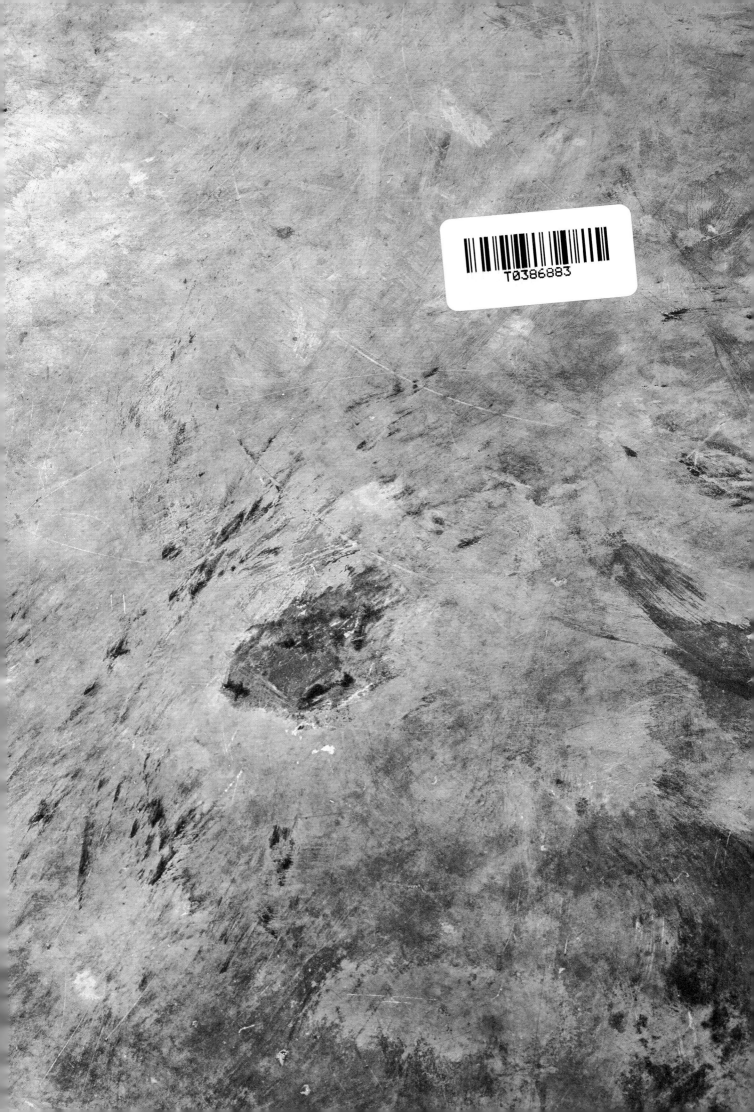

Vibrations

Published with support from:

dreyersfond

Karsten R.S. Ifversen
Photos by Jens Markus Lindhe

A Portrait of Houses Designed by
Lundgaard & Tranberg Architects

Vibrations

Contents

Foreword 7

An introductory essay
Vibrations 9
Phenomenology 13
Atmosphere 15
Time 21
Nature 23

The Wedge 25
The Tietgen Hall of Residence 55
**The Playhouse
and Kvæsthus Pier** 83

About the drawing office 130

Sorø Art Museum 138
SEB 156
The Villa in Hellerup 186
The Warehouse at Langelinie 216
Axel Towers 239

A concluding essay
The open programme 257
Far out in the forest 261
The eye, the body and the community 266

Literature 271

Foreword

Which is Denmark's best drawing office?

Considering how superficial the question is, it is one I am often asked. This kind of ranking seems populist and silly, because it is not possible to make such direct comparisons among drawing offices – as it is, for example, among manufacturers of chocolate, watches or cars, lots of which are made for the same purpose. But even in this case it is hard to say. One car maker may make the best middle-class family car and another the best sports car. Who is best?

There are so many more variables in architecture that only make it harder to compare the drawing offices behind the works. As a rule architect-designed buildings are only made in one instance for specific purposes and for a particular place. Circumstances vary from case to case, and how does one compare a public kindergarten with a private commercial project? Clients, financing and the planning basis vary each time, so one need not look far to see how hard the question can actually be to answer.

All the same, my answer comes promptly, for the name of one drawing office in particular comes up again and again when I have to point to the most successful and significant projects of the past decade and, perhaps not surprisingly for the reader of this book, the name of that drawing office is Lundgaard & Tranberg Arkitekter.

People – family, friends and colleagues – often come to me bursting with enthusiasm to talk about a new building they have experienced. It's quite fantastic, much better than everything else, and why isn't all new architecture like that? They have personally felt the power inherent in good architecture. Afterwards I can infer from their descriptions that it is SEB, the Tietgen Hall of Residence or the Playhouse they have experienced. But when I mention who is responsible, there is rarely any look of recognition in their eyes. Perhaps this book will help to ensure that the name of Lundgaard & Tranberg Arkitekter will be deservedly associated with their buildings, but that is not its intention.

At present Denmark has an ebullient architectural scene with many small and medium-sized firms and a few larger ones whose services have become sought after abroad. Danish architecture is a commercial success, but in addition to simply being an exportable commodity, the buildings of Lundgaard & Tranberg demonstrate a thoroughness and a search for long-term, sustainable qualities that one only finds to a lesser extent in other parts of the otherwise highly successful Danish architectural scene.

The firm's own focus is on the creation of architecture, and the promotion of its activities is confined to their website. For the most part one hears about them in interviews in books, periodicals and newspapers, and the client has had a monograph written about the Tietgen Hall of Residence. There is no independent book that gathers up the strands of the work of the firm. The present publication means to remedy this. But it is not to fill a gap in the bookshelf that I am writing this book.

My encounters with their projects have influenced my approach to architecture. In a way they are architecture's counterpart to Restaurant Noma. They take their point of departure in a Nordic tradition and the conditions of the place, but their will to renew architecture transcends the merely local and places them in a class with some of the world's leading drawing offices. Their best projects have equipped me with pointers and architectural touchstones, inasmuch as the consistency, detail and atmosphere of their buildings are qualities I hope to find in others.

That is why the aim of this book is not just a portrait; it is as much a personal clarification. I am trying to comprehend what it is about these buildings that makes me answer unhesitatingly that Lundgaard & Tranberg is the most important Danish drawing office of the time. If that is of interest to you, do read on.

Although I have worked with the interpretation and criticism of architecture for many years, I am not an architect. I have a master's in philosophy and the analysis of modern culture, and for the past twenty years and more I have worked to disseminate and review literature, art and architecture in a newspaper.

So there will undoubtedly be areas where the more architecturally knowledgeable will find that I neglect interesting aspects. My perspective on architecture is neither wider nor narrower than I express here; it is solely about my exploration of what is in play in the succession of notable buildings that I have selected.

I concentrate on works delivered within the past ten or more years, during which the projects of Lundgaard & Tranberg Arkitekter have taken a more nature-inspired and landscape-oriented turn. But this also coincides with the period when I have held the position as *Politiken*'s architecture editor and have therefore had a professional interest in investigating their architecture.

Any nonsense, inaccuracies and errors are the responsibility of the author. Unless otherwise indicated, the book only expresses the opinions of the writer. It has not been written to advertise Lundgaard & Tranberg Arkitekter, nor has it been commissioned by them. On the contrary, the drawing office is probably anticipating it with a certain trepidation. Nevertheless – or perhaps for that very reason – its partners have been very generous with their time and knowledge in several background interviews, and for this I thank them.

Karsten R.S. Ifversen, Copenhagen 2016

An introductory essay

Vibrations

In the author Svend Aage Madsen's novel *Af sporet er du kommet* ('Off the Track You Have Come'), the main character, Tøger, meets an author, Rikkard Duebo Vem, who does not write books. He doesn't need to, Rikkard thinks, because there are already enough novels out there. His authorship is of another kind; he has discovered that the works of world literature begin to glow if you put them in a special order. The walls in Rikkard's apartment are lined with books from floor to ceiling, and the apartment has subdued, even, pleasant lighting that comes from the bookshelves. The explanation, he claims to the gaping Tøger, is that they are all connected, not only symbolically but in reality too. A girl character in one book by Jane Austen is a little younger than but otherwise the same as one in Boccaccio. How it works he does not reveal, but he demonstrates that all works in particular editions are connected by some kind of internal wiring. If you remove a book or swap two around, the light dims. When they stand in the best way, they shine the brightest.

This sort of idea – that there is an order in the world where everything falls into place, where the whole becomes greater than the sum of the parts – is also a recurring metaphor when the founding partner of the firm, Lene Tranberg, talks about the architecture of her drawing office. When she talks about the creative process where all the detailed requirements in a construction project must result in an atmosphere, a narrative and an approach that give the building its materiality and form, she mentions the feeling for finding exactly the state in which the elements begin to 'vibrate'.

From this perspective the aim of architecture is not only to satisfy as many objective spatial requirements of the project as possible – demands made in the first instance by client, authorities and residents, and in the last analysis by the construction programme, engineers and contractors. It is not enough that the architecture is delivered on time, on budget and as an empty shell can serve the programmed functions. The architectural arrangement must first and foremost feel right; it must be sustained by an atmosphere that permeates the bodies of the users of the building and makes its connections with the surroundings shine.

Lundgaard & Tranberg Arkitekter's works have been formed with this conscious effort to make all the elements of the architecture merge in a vibrant totality. Partner Peter Thorsen says that they can sometimes sit drawing and redrawing one detail for years. It is perhaps not difficult to make a building viable, he says; to make it express an overall idea at the same time, however, is a whole craft in itself. But it is also an instrument for reaching awareness. Through the eternal redrawing and scrutiny of the detail, they arrive at a clarification of the main concept; what is it they want, what mood is it to express when the handrail meets the concrete in that exact way? This search for constructional distinctiveness in the detail is only interesting because it can at the same time open up a path whereby they can arrive poetically and philosophically at the main concept.

The endeavour to find a state in which all the elements play together in the creation of a strong atmosphere is something we are used to finding in other arts. However many contrapuntal, dissonant, meaning-deconstructing, open or self-contradictory elements there may be in music, poetry or visual art when it is really good, it is as if the sequence of notes, sentences or colours falls into place and creates an atmosphere where everything stands there vibrantly.

Art will always be born into a time, a place and a framework of understanding that affords the occasion for it to enter the world – no work comes from nothing – but precisely if it is ordered such that the internal 'wiring' of the elements is connected up as in Rikkard Duebo Vem's book collection, the work may perhaps transcend its own time and endure. This quest for a harmony of the elements is thus more than just aesthetic satisfaction. It is also an effort to produce enduring value.

Endurance should be the primary quality for which any housebuilder strives – not only for the sake of the investment but also for the sake of the climate. According to the UN, buildings are responsible globally for 40 per cent of mankind's energy consumption, 40 per cent of resource consumption, one third of greenhouse gas emissions and 25 per cent of water consumption.

It is of course necessary to build solidly to allow for the climate of the place, but that is not a sufficient path to sustainability, as confirmed by the bunkers of the occupying forces from World War II up and down the west coast of Jutland. The only thing that seriously endures is that people perceive that a building has value for them, that they care *about* the building and therefore care *for* it. In this respect beauty is an important and perhaps the essential factor.

One can forgive a beautiful building much, and one will go a long way to preserve it and adapt it to new functions. But buildings that have no other value than being adapted to specific functions lose their value when the function becomes irrelevant, and they will be more susceptible to neglect and in the end demolition, which means that all the energy and the resources expended on the building will be wasted.

Beauty is a common feature of the works of Lundgaard & Tranberg Arkitekter. But not in any direct way. It is not like the seductive placeless beauty one experiences in the furnishings of the flagship shops of the luxury brands around the world. Nor is beauty something they talk about as a direct goal. It is rather a result of the process, of the energy and the many hours invested in making the elements vibrate.

And although one often finds a dramatization of contrasts in light and space – that facades are composed as three-dimensional exchanges with the surroundings, that they consistently use the materials' own colours, surfaces and juxtapositions and have a certain fondness for not covering up the structures but letting the skeletons of the buildings remain as internal landscapes – the vibrant qualities of the buildings cannot be summed up with these characteristics, just as one cannot characterize Miles Davis's music solely in terms of his use of wind instruments, long solos or improvisation.

None of these is wrong, but they mistake where the nerve of the architecture and the music lie, in the organization of the elements, the interaction, which in the architecture of Lundgaard & Tranberg is also an interplay with the surroundings that changes from project to project.

It applies to all art that it is a composition of materials. The art of poetry is the composition of sentences and words. Visual art is the composition of symbols, motifs and colours. Music is the composition of notes in sequences. In all cases they work at several levels simultaneously, and the best works will probably always be those where one experiences a correspondence between the levels, a context within which the elements vibrate.

Architecture is seen as an applied art. This means that, more so than poetry and visual art, its works are subject to social and physical factors that are not under the control of the practitioner.

The architect is a consultant, and the contributions of many different people must fit together before the architecture can succeed. So of course it does not work equally well every time. But the projects that have been selected in this book all in one way or another have powerfully convincing atmospheres. They all seem to give more back to the place and life in the city than they take – as we can say with a slight reformulation of Lundgaard & Tranberg's motto at their website. They are generous.

It is my impression that neither the drawing office nor other artists for that matter have a formula for when something vibrates. It is something one must seek each time in the creative process and which one of course gets better at when one has tried it several times and acquired a feeling for where to look.

I do not think, either, that by trying to name all the elements that make up a work, one gets the totality to vibrate for the reader, but once one has noted that the work vibrates, one can go backwards and point out some of the elements that play together in it.

Tøger in the novel sees the light when the books of Rikkard Duebo Vem are set up in a particular way. And I note that the projects selected in this book all have an ordering of their elements that makes them vibrate.

Phenomenology

The philosopher Martin Heidegger says in the lecture 'The origin of the work of art' that the artwork is the rift in the world that opens up for us and renders visible what was formerly hidden. In principle all worked objects can be artworks, but he mentions specific examples of paintings, engravings, poems and architecture. An artwork is an intervention in the world that does something in particular through its mode of being. He mentions how a Greek temple at the top of a mountain evokes the 'mountain-ness' of the mountain for us. That sounds mystical, but, put in a more rationally humanist and rather less poetic way, it means that architecture's known human aspect, its comprehensible scale and proportions are made by and for us who relate the non-humanness and scale of the mountain to ourselves.

The interesting thing is the duality of the relation. Heidegger talks about how the temple sanctifies the mountain. On the one hand the temple incorporates it in our circle of awareness, our world; on the other the sanctification acknowledges the mountain as something else, something that belongs to the world of the gods.

The point here is thus that it is not the temple that is the artwork; it is the relation between the temple and the mountain. It is what the temple does to the mountain that is the art. It is this understanding of the connectedness of architecture with its surroundings that is the essence of the phenomenological tradition in architecture.

In Roman times it was thought that a spirit presided over a place, the *genius loci*, and that it was the housebuilder's task to please that spirit. The idea lived on in the Renaissance but was lost in modern times and disappeared entirely with modernism after World War II. Heidegger was the first to take up the concept and reinterpret it as an existential condition. He says that living somewhere means that one feels that one's world is meaningful. Later, architectural phenomenology was developed by, among others, the Italian architect Aldo Rossi, with studies of time and memory in the urban context, and the Norwegian architect Christian Norberg-Schultz's ideas about the *genius loci*, which exerted much influence in the 1980s at the School of Architecture of the Royal Danish Academy of Fine Arts, where Boje Lundgaard taught and Lene Tranberg was his pupil.

The phenomenological thought that there are special relations between the place and its buildings permeates the works of Lundgaard & Tranberg Arkitekter. The relationship with the surroundings can be understood – with a comparison from physics – as the relationship between waves and resonance. If one's intervention is in phase with the oscillations of the place, a strong impact can be achieved with very little effort, but if one works out of phase with the vibrations of the place, however much force, materials and money one applies, the benefit becomes less despite the effort. Investigating the potential of a place, listening to its possibilities and giving it detailed thought before one intervenes is – also at the purely practical level – a way of economizing with one's energy. But in the longer term the important thing is whether one evokes stories, connections and topographies that have hitherto lain as unknown potentials.

This idea of trying to build for, please or evoke the spirit of a place may sound to modern ears like magic and mysticism. Heidegger's talk of the temple sanctifying the mountain may sound like something that belongs to the spiritual practices of a premodern world. But in our time it turns out to be a way of recognizing that one cannot simply reduce architecture to a form of engineering, where a building is seen as an independent technical solution to the need to cover a particular number of square metres.

In place-conscious phenomenological architecture one works for an awareness that there are already historical, spatial and aesthetic associations at the place. These associations are not confined to the building site that has been marked out or the local plan that has to be implemented. In a city or a landscape there is a topography and a past one can play along with or play against. It takes a musical mind and an architectural responsiveness to both sense and play on these associations. They go far beyond the building in question, but if one is attentive, one feels them immediately as a background resonance that the work invokes as it draws on connections larger than itself.

Examples of how Lundgaard & Tranberg Arkitekter's buildings evoke the spirit of the place are legion: a round hall of residence in a neighbourhood that is dominated by parallel-bar-like buildings secures the lines of the place, which otherwise all lead away from it. A bank headquarters steps to one side and is split up into two protective walls around a public space in an otherwise heavily trafficked neighbourhood full of buildings that puff themselves up. A project for a large city building with offices and businesses is split up into a cluster of round towers that draw on a long-forgotten story of the fortifications of the city and give beauty and amenity values to a place in the city that has hitherto been without them.

The buildings are derived from conditions and possibilities that existed precisely at the places where they are built. To use the image from wave physics, they have a positive interference with the vibrations of the places. These can be topographic, historical or social in nature, and preferably all of these at once. Deepest down it is from this care with the adaptation to the surroundings that the buildings gain their generosity. They work not only for themselves but for an area.

As with Heidegger's temple on the mountain, the phenomenological understanding of architecture is about the fact that in the end, if one understands a project properly, one does not necessarily have to do so much. Care in the analysis pays off. One only has to lay a few stones one on top of another to make a whole mountain shine.

Atmosphere

Lene Tranberg says that when they begin work on a project, it always starts as a sensation, as a feeling: 'We always think of architecture as atmosphere, something one tries to concentrate and complete. It is about listening to a place, finding the music and the energy that flow through everything. This is where it starts. The difficult thing is how you convert this into a building. It begins with the sense of a saturated atmosphere which we only slowly begin to translate into substance, structure, light and shade. It is truly interesting to see how, in the Playhouse as in other cases, it has set all the spaces in motion and filled out all its layers of differences, as different degrees of concentration in the atmosphere. The whole house comes from the same grain of sand.'

The atmosphere – with the definite article – is the layer of air around the Earth. It is essential to life, and we cannot spend much time in a space empty of air. When we speak of atmosphere in architecture, it is a metaphor that carries over some of these meanings.

In the space age, when mankind seriously began to explore the empty space outside the atmosphere, the architects of Earth had ever since the Renaissance become used to thinking of architecture as the art of forming space. Surfaces and lines were seen as the constituent elements in this fundamentally mathematical-geometrical art. But the abstract concept of space lacks what makes a place habitable for human beings. And this is where atmosphere comes into the picture.

The word is used in everyday language as a synonym for the mood or feeling of a place, but although the concepts all have to do with us as sensuous and sensing beings, it is practical to separate them here.

We know about being in love, about being filled up inside with a feeling. It is as if your chest is bursting with the thought of the one you love. Feelings take place inside the body and can fill it up completely. But moods do not only exist inside you; they are about the interplay of the mind with other people.

You may have felt the silence that descends when you sit at a meeting and are told that someone is to be sacked. When the mood in a room becomes tense enough it is said that you could cut the air with a knife. And surely everyone has experienced how the spirits are lifted when you enter a party where everyone is simply happy. In that sense moods are not feelings that only exist within ourselves. They are something we are put in.

But it is not only the mood among people that affects us. Our physical surroundings do it too. When we leave a bar with friends, we agree that the place had a good atmosphere, when it is not just the atmosphere among ourselves we are thinking of, although that has played a part in the perception. The experience of the atmosphere of a place involves something that lies outside the interpersonal mood; it is about the relationship between us and the place.

If on a warm summer day in Rome you have stepped into a dark, chilly church interior, you know that it is more than just the temperature that has changed. It is the scale, the history and the care that has been used to create the interior that strikes you. You encounter it all at once. It is a special atmosphere.

Similarly, there is a special atmosphere in a dense forest, on a beach, in a cave, in a gym and in an airport. All interiors have an atmosphere; it lies there, thick or thin, unavoidable and everywhere, and follows from the combination of colours, smells, sound and all the dispositions of the senses, memories, recollections, ideas and expectations we ourselves bring into the room.

Atmosphere is thus neither an objective relationship between objects, a mood among people, nor a purely subjective feeling in the individual. But the fact that atmosphere is experienced individually does not mean that it is random or just a matter of taste. The atmosphere of a room is experienced in much the same way by people from the same background and cultural circle. It is a relationship between us, our history and the physical surroundings, and it affects our well-being.

In recent years phenomenologically-minded architects have become increasingly attentive to atmosphere. The Swiss architect Peter Zumthor, viewed by many as a pioneer in the field, published a lecture he gave in 2003 about his activities, entitled 'Atmospheres', and research is being done widely on the concept, even though in the nature of things it is hard to pin down. For atmosphere cannot be restricted to a few aspects like space, scale, light, acoustics, proportions, materials, assemblies, or whatever may keep architects occupied on a daily basis. Atmosphere is a totality; it is all of this at once and yet none of it, for it is a relationship that lies between us and our surroundings.

As Lene Tranberg puts it:

'Juhani Pallasmaa, Gaston Bachelard and Merleau-Ponty point out how as a human being one senses a place with one's whole body. It has something to do with the atmosphere, the mood and the sound of the space, the room's own oscillations. What is it that is happening, how is it manifested? Already before you register the details, you have a sense of it. And I have realized that our programme for designing architecture is about that. We programme things according to an atmosphere we are expected to be able to establish, and we talk about that before we talk about the form, the materials and the structures. It is the mood in relation to the people and the place that we begin to home in on, all the way from the outside, instead of just looking purely locally. And then we zoom in and out again.'

Although atmosphere is inevitably present in any space, it does not affect us in any direct physical way in the same way as gravity holds us down, roofs protect us, walls separate and doors let us in or out. But it works in the mind, so not everyone is affected equally by atmosphere, nor is one always even affected by it.

Atmosphere is about presence. Our body is after all always present, but we are not always present in our own body. We can often have our minds in a quite different place – and fortunately so.

We can ignore a bad atmosphere; we can ignore that we are sitting in a prison cell with only a small window out to the sky. But only for a while. For we cannot detach the mind from the body, as the phenomenologist Maurice Merleau-Ponty pointed out. They are two sides of the same thing.

Uncomfortable places drain us, whether they are consciously thought of as such or are only the result of different interests, or perhaps of no one giving the matter any thought. We expend energy ignoring the atmosphere; on the other hand we can be strengthened by the energy that is latent in a good atmosphere – not that it should sound like a lifestyle project to optimize one's atmosphere.

What is interesting for an architect to know is where the atmosphere starts. It is something we feel intuitively – with the emphasis on *feel*.

The building is not seen simply as an anonymous framework for human activities; its mode of being affects us morally. In the frieze of C.F. Hansen's courthouse in Copenhagen we can read 'With law shall the land be built.' But the words would not seem convincing if looking at the pediment had not already made us stand up straight. The weight and majestic proportions of the Ionic columns radiate power, order and plenitude. Our minds are reflected in the surroundings because we experience them with our bodies.

We engage in an exchange with buildings that is not causal, but an exchange of meaning. We read the city and its buildings with the body. Great mass and dense spaces can have a threatening or reassuring effect. Lightness and open spaces can have a liberating or agitating effect. The meanings depend on the context.

The surroundings offer themselves as physical signs in an interpretative tradition and as invitations to action. A bench in a city space is not an abstract form, it is an invitation to sit down, and on seeing it we mentally engage in a lightning-fast negotiation – is it comfortable, does it have a good sitting height and is it clean enough? – regardless of whether we are tired and need to sit down or not. The city space is experienced as more caring when it shows with a bench that it is not only intended for passage. If you need to, you can sit down, the city tells us. This banal example has only been used to demonstrate how phenomenology can claim that the bodily interpretation of the world precedes any abstract reading of the surroundings. In our fast-accelerating late modern society, where we cycle, drive a car or take a train and are often deeply preoccupied with a digital flow of images, we see most of the world through the eyes; the other senses are put on standby when we are in fast motion, but we still interpret what we see with the body.

Buildings that have a particularly powerful atmosphere often give me associations with food. I described the round Tietgen Hall of Residence in my original newspaper review as a layer cake, and the dark bricks of the Playhouse reminded me at the same time of a rye loaf, coffee and chocolate. When I have talked to the photographer for the book, Jens Lindhe, about the Warehouse at Langelinie, we have referred to it either as 'the loaf' for its shape or 'the cheese' for its holes.

Architecture can offer bodily stimuli through the sense of vision, which works together with other senses in a so-called *synaesthesia*. Not all buildings have that effect, and not every time. Unlike atmosphere, synaesthesia is not a semi-objective phenomenon, but it is not strictly subjective either. The comparisons become meaningful to communicate because the encounter with the atmosphere the buildings put us in is related to sensory experiences one has had with one's mouth, and these have a special priority in our development. After all, the mouth is the first organ of the senses with which a baby explores and discovers its world. But that does not mean that the world comes to us in small sensory morsels.

In his book *Truth and Method* from 1960, Hans-Georg Gadamer combines Heidegger's phenomenology with the interpretative discipline of hermeneutics. His point in it is that we never experience the world around us being pieced together bit by bit. The world, on the contrary, is always whole, complete and enveloping. It can then be adjusted piece by piece by linear, stringent investigations of its factual state, but always in order to return to a new understanding of the totality. In the science of interpretation this is called the hermeneutic circle. The existential point for Gadamer is that there is no point outside the circle; the parts always refer to the whole and vice versa. We know only the world we have before us, and any investigation of its nature must be based on prior judgements we project from our previous experience of the world. This means that for Gadamer pre-judging becomes a necessary and positive concept. We are constantly positing new judgements about the nature of the world, and as we see in the work of Merleau-Ponty this takes place in bodily exchanges. When we encounter a building, our body creates images of it – rather in the same way as we form complete images of people we have just met. We think of someone who does not greet us as arrogant or shy, even though we have only met that person once. We inevitably think that their inner nature is reflected in their outer nature, whether this is the case or not.

Buildings, despite their considerable size, can seem pleasant and soothingly crowded in their scale, as is the case, for example, with Lundgaard & Tranberg's residential project Havneholmen, which with all its projections and protuberances recalls something that has grown up over time. Or they can seem powerful and perhaps threatening like C.F. Hansen's Courts of Justice. Mankind's proportions are always embedded in architecture, but whether the effect is daunting or disarming has much to do with the proportions. We see it with our eyes but our bodies tell us how we feel about it.

The Finnish architect and theoretician Juhani Pallasmaa argues in his book *The Eyes of the Skin: Architecture and the Senses* against the architecture that only wants to create pictures and scenery instead of an architecture that is experienced with the whole body: the hand that feels the banister, the muscular tension in the legs on ascending the staircase and the upper body that puts its weight into opening the door. The bodily approach to architecture is about the way the quality of architecture primarily lies elsewhere than the qualities reached through the eye.

Juhani Pallasmaa uses the nest-building of the bird as an example of a bodily phenomenological approach to architecture. It shapes its nest with its body and thus ensures that it fits. Our well-being, he points out, is in the long run tied to the sense of touch, not to what impresses the eye.

With the bird example he wants to point out not only that the body precedes vision but also that the art-historical approach to architecture which focuses on styles in terms of changing facade features is quite literally superficial.

We do not only experience buildings with our bodies. We also experience them as if they are themselves bodies, where the structure forms the skeleton, windows are eyes and facades are skin. Doors are bodily orifices, piping is veins and the intestinal system, and wiring is nerves. This is a cognitive disposition that the visual artists Randi and Katrine explore and exploit in their installations. This intimate relationship with the body is not something architects explore if they see architecture as abstract spaces or simply as impressive sculptures.

But the fact that one perceives the atmosphere through one's bodily presence does not mean that one has to believe that such an atmosphere is created just by making the available materials appetizing, by finding the right piece of wood, a raw concrete wall and a leather-wound banister that can together create a nice, congenial interior, as a one-sided understanding of Palasmaa's points might indicate. It is about making these details vibrate in a larger resonating space than the one immediately before you. Lene Tranberg explains the perspective in terms of music:

'When Mahler wrote his Creation Symphony, he thought of the becoming of the world as he did so. And you can hear that there is more at stake than him thinking that it sounded good when he placed the notes against one another. It was a much larger world he was grasping at. When we are in architecture we like, it is those narratives we can feel. Someone has made an effort to give us something more than just a frame, a door and a handle. There is a narrative of the whole of existence if we take a little more trouble to listen for it.'

Time

Sand, clay, wood and metal worked in various ways are the precondition of almost all construction. But it is rare that one actually feels the strength of the steel, the weight of the masonry and the growth in the wood when one moves around in a new building. What keeps the house standing, its construction, is as a rule hidden behind several layers of insulation and plasterboard, while the exterior has a protective facade with certain quite different qualities.

False ceilings conceal the building's whole intestinal system of sewage pipes, its nervous system of electric wiring and its lungs for ventilation. So the rooms we live and move in are detached from the skeletons that bear them. In the Danish climate one cannot simply have a light, open structure. One has to build thick walls, and legislation decides how much daylight there has to be at the very least and how much the heat loss may be. As a rule this leads to many layers of clothing and is a challenge to the dream of a house that quite nakedly and plainly speaks of its own construction.

From traditional half-timbering through modern Scandinavian furniture art to the concrete Brutalism of the 1970s, it has been seen as a virtue and a heritage in Nordic design to show the construction. It is considered particularly frugal and honest to show how the constructive and the functional are combined, that one uses the materials with care and that the solutions fit elegantly. It is like mathematics. One can find many ways of solving a problem, but the shortest one is considered best. A certain beauty is inherent in the simple and the clear, in transparency. But this is also an expression of a design tradition that has grown up in a region with scarce resources. More traditionally prosperous regions have given rise to a decorative understanding of beauty where bricks are never left bare and a layer of decoration is seen as a necessary termination.

In the works of Lundgaard & Tranberg one experiences this Nordic heritage in the way the expression of atmosphere is always sought in a corresponding constructional rigour. Ideally, by looking at the proportion of a building one can get an idea of its construction and its internal spaces when the attempt has been made to articulate all the elements clearly, from the overall idea through the use of materials to how they are joined together. The structure must explain itself, nothing must be pushed in beneath a concealing plate, but in practice lots of technology is hidden away in floors or ceiling. Constructional honesty in architecture will always only be a utopia one strives for. But the endeavour helps to show the building as something that is built. The actual time the construction process takes is embedded in the building when one can see how the layers differ from one another.

The choice of materials and the details of the assembly thus show the role played by the element in the building, and it is rare to see painted surfaces in the firm's buildings. It is the materials' own aesthetic qualities, and not least their natural decay, their patina, that create the atmosphere.

But this will to articulate the various parts, their role in the building and their conditioning by time differs from the design philosophy that comes to expression in projects by other successful Danish architectural firms, such as Henning Larsen, 3XN and Schmidt Hammer Lassen. These three work with three different design philosophies, but they have a more seamless, minimalist and crystalline design in common. Their aim is to give the users a sense of being transported into pure, timeless spatialities, often ethereal states with white surfaces and few but striking spatial effects. This can give their buildings a certain resemblance to cars – ideally they must be polished and cared for and, if not repainted, at least after some years have their interiors painted and facades replaced so as to look as clean as when they were conceived.

Lundgaard & Tranberg's buildings on the other hand often appear dark and intended only to be made more beautiful by standing in wind and weather. Surfaces of brick, wood, copper and tombac have their own fullness from the outset, but they also patinate and change colour. These are materials that display their ageing, their slow journey back to nature, to sand, stone, clay and metal.

Nature

In a landscape there are no walls. There are states, densities and openings, but everywhere there is one and the same open space. In recent years this kind of spatiality has taken on greater and greater significance in the works of Lundgaard & Tranberg Arkitekter.

The relationship between landscape and building has been a central point of interest since Boje Lundgaard's first projects in the 1970s but over the past ten years has become a truly new kind of architectural space formation where nature's way of condensing and opening up space has been transferred into the arrangement of several of their buildings. They now see themselves as much as landscape architects as building architects and have thus joined an international trend that also includes names like Norwegian Snøhetta and Japanese Sanaa.

There are still some fundamental differences between the 'grown' and the 'built', as they are called by the landscape architect Stig L. Andersson, but in recent years there has been a rapprochement between the two disciplines. Landscape art has escaped the confines of the garden and park as the fenced-in ideal conception of nature. It has become a practical, functional discipline involved both in solving climatic problems and creating recreative amenity values in the cities. And the art of building in most of the Lundgaard & Tranberg works discussed in this book is spatially and functionally inspired by an unbounded mode of existence not necessarily determined by optimization for a single function.

More than anything, the space of nature not only has a function; it is multifunctional and can do all sorts of things in one and the same place. In this nature-inspired architectural thinking the aim is on the one hand to create something not only for the primary user but also for whoever is just passing by, or those we do not yet know about but who will come to use the building for something quite different in many years' time; on the other hand it is also about giving architecture a new dignity and authority that it lost in its Functionalist uniformity.

Many buildings, factories and ships are determined by their functions. But nature is not monofunctional. It is free in its openness to interpretation, as Lene Tranberg puts it:

'Nature has no boundaries; it does not stop anywhere. It is from nature we draw our greatest inspiration; it has an inherent vibration, a kind of crispness one rarely finds in architecture.

Even in the most barren season nature is never ugly. You are never put in a bad mood by going for a walk in natural surroundings. But I can be by walking in a bleak place in the city. Nature has its energy in all its layers, and you intuitively sense being one with it. And it is interesting if one can create an architecture that can draw on some of those vibrations.'

'When you look at visual art, read literature and hear music, you are sure that the artists are on to something, and no one doubts that this is so. Architecture has simply lost out in this sense because we believed it was at a more technical level that we had to justify ourselves. Now we are about to reconquer the terrain. Perhaps it hasn't really started yet. The next generation will unfurl it all in a quite different way. We're only sniffing around the beginning.'

Partner in the drawing office Henrik Schmidt imagines that one day people may reach the point where they can create spaces they do not know what to use for but which must first be explored and discovered like a new landscape. Places where you burst out: 'Wow, there can be a great library here,' or 'I can live here.' Stepping right out of functionalism.

As Lene Tranberg adds: 'Yes, in fact, what is space at all – what do we want to do with it?'

The Wedge

In the works of Lundgaard & Tranberg Arkitekter it has always been possible to see a special preoccupation with the encounter between building and surroundings. They bring out a special character in the surroundings, just as Heidegger points out that a temple can evoke the mountain on which it stands. But the exchange between building and surroundings does not only take place in the grand lines; it is also very close in the transition between inside and outside. In the Danish climate there are limits to how open one can make one's buildings. But the interweaving with the surroundings of the buildings in terms of landscape, society and history is something that is manifested in a new way in the educational building Kilen (The Wedge) in Frederiksberg.

The Wedge was completed in 2006 and is enthroned high above its area. With its surrounding mounds, undercut base and coloured shutters it has something of the character of a stylized grove of trees that is broken up by the soil and stands shimmering with its shutters in the colours of autumn leaves.

The new town centre in Frederiksberg

The Wedge is part of CBS, Copenhagen Business School, a commercial university with 20,000 students, 2,000 staff and a campus with many addresses around Frederiksberg. At such a distributed institution it is difficult to create a sense of unity of the type known from the Copenhagen University Faculty of Natural Sciences on Nørre Alle with its many buildings around an inner park.

But it was just such a composition that Lundgaard & Tranberg Arkitekter created along with the firm Marianne Levinsen Landskab for the commercial university on the former track of the Frederiksberg railway station, consolidating several buildings and institutes around a common landscape intersected by walking and cycling paths.

Today the area is still marked by the fact that the surroundings earlier had their back to the railway. And it does not make it any easier that even recent projects like the Frederiksberg Centre by KHR, Frederiksberg High School by Henning Larsen Architects and the renovated central library are mainly inward-facing buildings with closed facades towards the campus area.

Vilhelm Lauritzen Architects designed the first stage of the new campus area of the Business School, the Business Economic Faculty Solbjerg Plads, which was completed in 2000. This is a rather rigorous structuralist building of parallel bars tied together by a transverse inner street and with a facade motif that rather curiously, and probably arbitrarily, refers to the Faaborg

District Heating Plant by Lundberg & Tranberg Arkitekter. But along with a gable opening in the Frederiksberg Centre the building forms a frame around the new square Solbjerg Plads, which has given its name to the department.

This new inward orientation did not in itself seriously change the sense that the space had been left over from an urban process that had sent marginal development in all other directions. But its mixed character did become a creative starting point for the landscape design office SLA's reworking of the urban space that is now called the new Frederiksberg town centre. SLA has divided up the scale of this first stage of the campus into five areas of very different, highly concentrated atmospheres between the mall, the high school, the library and the business school. In the middle stand pine trees on a hilly grass landscape; between the high school and the library stand leafy trees and hedges in squared-off areas with hard, rusted corten steel edges, and in front of the school is a large square with water vapour from jets and natural sound from speakers hidden in the cladding. On the square there is a giant basin with highly varied planting and a kerb one can sit on. Room has also been made for a waterfall with a 'starry sky' behind it in a retaining wall. The landscape spaces have helped to create attractions for those who pause and pass by in the new town centre.

The next stage was to form an overall plan for the development of the campus as well as a building with new teaching and research facilities, and it was this contract that Lundgaard & Tranberg Arkitekter won along with Marianne Levinsen Landskab. Solbjerg Plads was tied together with new additions to the school towards the west. The solution was to create a more homogeneous open park area with groves and freestanding structures that stood like pavilions in the landscape. This was 'garden thinking' in the midst of what was otherwise a dense urban context but as such is not unusual for Frederiksberg, which originally grew up around a castle and its park and later as a green residential neighbourhood outside the walls of Copenhagen.

This starting point in the understanding of the place as a green landscape rather than the more urban character that the earlier development had pointed towards has given Lundgaard & Tranberg Arkitekter's educational building The Wedge its special atmosphere, where the architecture is interwoven with the landscape.

Facade like autumn leaves

The Wedge appears from the outside as a stacking of its functions. It contains teaching localities and study facilities in the lower levels and researchers' offices on the upper floors. The soft landscape-like base bears an undercut floor, above which are four floors with shutters. The shutters can be turned individually around a vertical axis, and with its random variations of materials and colour shades the building is one of the first examples of a showdown with the more homogeneous and monotonous facade systems that had hitherto typified Danish buildings and which one sees, for example, in Vilhelm Lauritzen Arkitekter's square Solbjerg Plads.

A precursor for a more living facade system can be seen in 3XN's office block built for the former credit institution FIH Bank from 2002 at Langelinie, where white shutters can be slid aside and cover the red facade. This produces a building that changes its appearance and colour according to the day, the season and its current use. The reversible shutters of The Wedge also make the facade changeable, and they enter into a dialogue with the colours of the city and the park in oak, green matte glass and reddish copper in an arbitrary combination that always gives the facade a calmly crowded appearance, like foliage in unassuming autumn colours.

The mobility of the facade is part of the air conditioning, where light and heat can be adjusted locally as required. Along with the organic mobility that gives the facade its depth, there is also something rail-like in the horizontally accentuated lines to which the shutters are attached. This gives The Wedge a perhaps unintended reference to the earlier use of the place as the terminus of the Frederiksberg railway line, and to the Metro, which now runs silently beneath the landscape.

The mechanical, industrial and infrastructural in the construction runs like a track that can be read off in many of the works of the drawing office, along with the increasing inspiration from nature. Here nature, history and infrastructure support the architecture and vice versa such that the atmosphere of the place becomes a sense of strata formed by the different life flows that pass under and around the building, the slower ones that go through it and the absolutely calm flows of life on the staircases and study in the offices.

Atrium houses everywhere

The Wedge has been built as an atrium or courtyard building, a type of building which at the beginning of the 2000s had become the typical solution for commerce and education. As a rule these were large, deep boxes with glass facades that required external sun screens with slats. They appeared everywhere to meet all requirements, because they are rational and energy-effective in the Danish climate. Atrium houses can contain many square metres with a minimal surface – and despite the depth, the interior light well that gives the building type its name provides sufficient borrowed daylight. Contemporary examples of the type are Henning Larsen Architects' office hotel on Strandvejen in Tuborg Nord, 3XN's headquarters for the accountancy firm Deloitte on Amager Boulevard or Lundgaard & Tranberg

Arkitekter's building for the Danish tax and customs authority in Aalborg. They may all be excellent buildings, but it became something of a standard solution – by and large the architectural element was reduced to variations in the design of the stairs of the atria and the choice of material for the sun screens of the glass facades.

The Wedge grows far more organically out of its main narrative of the pavilion in the garden and the conditions of the building site with an underground Metro line, and surrounded by public walking and cycling paths.

Come into the woods

The landscape has the appearance of a green grassy surface intersected by a promenade in a straight line between The Wedge and Solbjerg Plads. The eight-metre-wide promenade is cast in a light brushed concrete where the surface has been given grooves by brushing it with a broom before it set. Over and above the practical factor that this makes the surface less slippery, the grooves create a relief and a sensory microscale for what would otherwise just be a surface – they are like the blades of a grassy lawn.

The straight line of the path is broken by an overlapping circular grove of copper beeches and by round beds that look like holes punched in the cladding, where tall white grasses pitch in the wind.

The ground plans of the promenade, the groves and the beds are laid one over the other: you cannot say whether the promenade goes through a grove or the surface of the promenade is perforated by beds. The hierarchy of the garden structures has been broken down to create a space of transit where you have to pay attention to where you put your feet, like when you walk in the woods. Groves and beds lower your walking speed and give a corresponding sensuousness to movement between the departments of the university.

The base of The Wedge is formed to communicate the flows of motion that surround the building. The foyer itself forms a lateral connection between the two surrounding path connections and leads to an older town house behind, which the drawing office has also transformed into teaching localities for the Business School.

The mounds around the footing cover the auditoria of the buildings. They are clad with grass which on the sun-facing south side often seems to have difficulty taking root. Just here it appears to be a challenge for the school to maintain the plantings. The earthworks cling around the building and on each long side become green seating stairs around the main entrances. And so the public landscape space continues in an unconfined motion towards the entrances and into the building.

The footing seems solid and protective, but it is also soil that is broken up by the force that lifts the building up, like roots that can raise the ground around a tree. It morphs into a building and staircase by the door, where it glides inside as a cast staircase that continues around the atrium and slips out through the door on the opposite side, where it again morphs into a mound. The mound, the grass and the glass surrounded by solid oak frames enter here into an intricate dynamic play of materiality, weight and direction in which the facade is minimized to a glass membrane that maintains the indoor climate.

In the atrium the building reveals its column-and-deck construction where all the columns and fronts of balconies appear in raw concrete. The ceilings are in white soundproofing plaster that takes a warm tone from the reflections of the balconies' red magnesite floors. The rails are quite minimal steel structures wound with light-coloured leather, so the building is warm and soft when you touch it. This makes the atrium light and elegant, while the atmosphere is warm.

It is a wonderful space. The daylight from above is dramatized by round wells that repeat the circles in the landscape outside, and from the sides it flows in through the glass walls of the offices, where it blends with the artificial lighting. The visual contact that the illumined offices make with the surroundings and the atrium balconies has, however, not proved entirely unproblematical for researchers who prefer to work untroubled by the gaze of others and in more enclosed working environments.

But the atmosphere is both inwardly unifying and openly permeable as in the grove outside. If you look down at the atrium floor from the balconies above, you see a black lake. The seating stairs are used both as places for studying and for assemblies. It is all cast in a mega-terrazzo created with large granite blocks. Boje Lundgaard is said to have had the idea for it when he was winter-bathing and saw large ice floes floating among one another.

But he never saw the building finished in 2005. He died on 19 April 2004 of a heart attack while the drawing office was in the midst of the work on their three most important projects so far: The Wedge, the Tietgen Hall of Residence and the Playhouse.

But the way The Wedge grows together with the landscape marked an innovative breakthrough, a new opening in the works of the firm. It is as if after this they have been more liberated from traditional building typologies and each time find new ways of interweaving with the surroundings, as in Ørestad, where the Tietgen Hall of Residence undertakes to heal a sick urban structure.

The Wedge

Address:
Kilevej 14, Frederiksberg

Area:
10,700 m^2

Client:
Copenhagen Business School (CBS)

Client's consultant:
EMCON A/S

Engineering:
Niras A/S

Landscaping:
Marianne Levinsen A/S
+ Algren and Bruun

Dates:
First Prize in project competition, 2002
Built in 2004-05

Awards:
RIBA European Award 2006
Frederiksberg Municipality 2006

Opening. In the evening it becomes quite clear how landscape and foyer have been conceived in a mutual relationship.

Gesture. The glass is only a climatic screen that the base of the building passes through. The function of the seating stairs is the same on both sides.

Chimney. The indoor climate is controlled by natural ventilation. Warm air rises in the atrium, and specially developed, automated louvres are built into the shell walls of the building.

Fullness. Magnesite floors give a warm tone to ceilings and walls, and leather-wound handrails make the building soft and pleasant to handle and show traces of use.

Podium. There are places to study on the seating stairs on the first floor in the atrium.

Flow. The giant terrazzo of the atrium floor continues up in the seating stairs, which have been given dark leather cushions for sitting comfort.

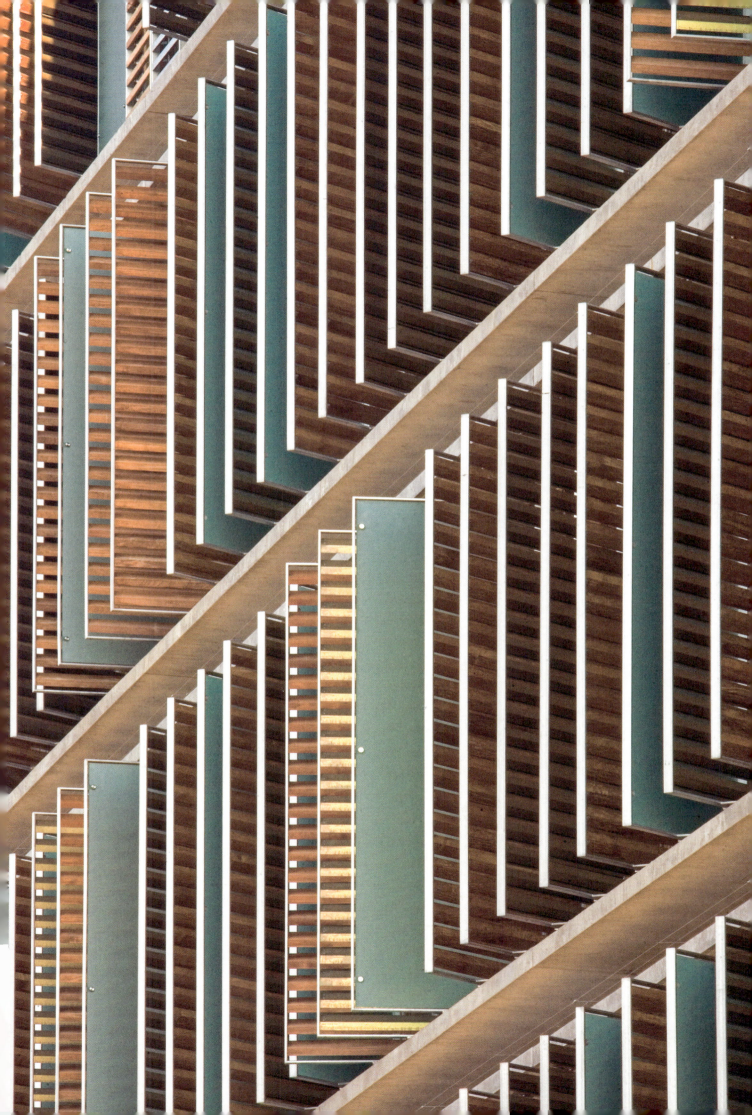

Tietgen Hall of Residence

The Tietgen Hall of Residence is a round building in Copenhagen's new neighbourhood Ørestad and is by far its most beautiful feature. It lies with a natural authority in an area that one otherwise feels has none and is an insistent, concentrating focus for the atmosphere of the place, which otherwise seems to leak along characterless facades out towards blind vanishing points. But first and foremost it functions as an intense social mechanism for its young residents.

Since it was planned in the 1990s Ørestad has been a driving force in the wide-ranging and successful effort to elevate the capital out of poverty and into the prosperity of the twenty-first century. For decades private commerce had given Copenhagen a wide berth. The capital lacked the large development areas and fast infrastructure that one found in the municipalities of the environs. Its new urban neighbourhood, sited on a five-kilometre-long narrow strip of the large nature reserve Amager Common, was to house exactly these features. It lay just beside the airport and was crossed by regional trains and the motorway and was further supported by a new bridge to Sweden. The Metro was dug down beneath the old city, while out in this 'new town' it was lifted proudly up as an overhead line. Ørestad and the Metro are simply two sides of the same thing. Sales of properties in Ørestad help to pay for the construction of the Metro, and the oblong neighbourhood is organized in four smaller sections each around its own station. The fast infrastructure is both its physical backbone and its selling point: you can get quickly to and from Ørestad.

But easy as that is, it is hard to bond with the place. The plan for Ørestad North created by the drawing offices KHR and Finnish Arkki was that the built-up areas would follow the Metro line in parallel like plough furrows. In the in many ways climatically prophetic project, rainwater canals were a crucial motif, and a central axis in Ørestad North is marked by Emil Holms Kanal flanked by a promenade. The surrounding projects for large educational institutions follow the canal like long bars.

But this gives the area a peculiar atmosphere, because all the lines in the urban space point away from the place, giving the impression that no one wants to hold on to you. The speed of the Metro has determined the design of the urban space and drawn the lines of its adjacent buildings. That was changed by the Tietgen Hall of Residence.

Better than your own apartment

The building was commissioned by the private foundation Nordea-fonden, whose board had noted that hardly any new student halls of residence had been built in the city for twenty years, and that in the 1990s students apparently preferred to live in cooperative condominium-type apartments, which at that time were inexpensive and plentiful in the old workers' neighbourhoods Nørrebro and Vesterbro. But the board could themselves remember the great importance of meeting other students in the hall-of-residence communities in their formative student years.

In other words they wanted to create a hall of residence where community values were central and which was so attractive that it could compete successfully with the dream of having one's own apartment. In the architectural competition no financial upper limit was imposed on the realization of the goal. It was up to the participants to find the best conceivable solution.

Nordea-fonden along with the Copenhagen City Council had picked out the location of the new hall of residence. The Faculty of Humanities at Copenhagen University was already in Ørestad North, and in 2004 the IT University would be opening, so it was an obvious choice to put a hall of residence where it could give the neighbourhood a life outside teaching hours and help to turn it into a new 'Latin Quarter'.

The site they picked out was wedge-shaped, in between two waterways: the straight, urban Emil Holms Kanal with hard edges and a promenade; and the landscape-like, winding rivulet flowing into the lake Grønjordssøen.

Collectivity as resistance

The local plan stipulated that the complex had to be given another wing or two if the building was to fit in between the parallel rows. But Lundgaard & Tranberg Arkitekter stuck its neck out and broke through the framework of the competition and the urban plan. The solution was not a wing. It was a circle.

The proposal required a change in the local plan, but neither the jury nor the city council were in any doubt that Lundgaard & Tranberg Arkitekter's suggestion was the right project for the place. Instead of a 'barred' project that followed the lines, they proposed to incorporate some of the promenade in the public space and go up close to Emil Holms Kanal. On the other hand the building would give more public space back and create a connection between the two canal spaces on either side. But in the first instance this approach perhaps established not so much a cohesiveness in the neighbourhood as a resistance to its lack of cohesion. It places a full stop in the middle of a smooth, unthinking flow of buildings that stand like words in a sentence with no point.

It is a refractory building which like a teenager does the opposite of the plan conceived for it. It refused to continue the modernist idea of the urban space as a function derived from the infrastructure. If it was to make sense that the place was for presence and movement, it had to be arranged in a way that offered a human response in a form that was, so to speak, worth going for. It found a gap in the urban plan and filled it.

Through its circular form and the baroque gesture of the facade it found its own way to bond with the place.

The Tietgen Hall of Residence's urban-aesthetic function is multiple. The building is a cork against the draining of energy brought about by the parallel lines. And the courtyard space is a clearance that creates a place where life can unfold. In this way its circle functions as an exclusion, a demarcation. In the competition submission the drawing office referred to, among other things, the Chinese Hakka people's round settlements and the ring forts of the Vikings. These were defensive works created as fortifications in a hostile landscape. The precondition for any community is after all always a demarcation and a separating-out of something. Community means that people create something together. But it is also a requirement for having something to share out. For that reason the architecture of the hall of residence should not be seen primarily as a circle but precisely as a community one steps into and out of. The hall of residence is not a closed, self-sufficient system. It is not a closed circle, and this very reciprocity with the surrounding world is its true motivation and the reason for its baroque facade design.

The hall of residence consists of five curved blocks separated by open balconies and stairwells with wisteria. The facade has balconies and cantilevered bays in deep relief. Like a stack of six staggered cogwheels it produces an intense dynamism. A bay on one floor leaves room for a balcony on the floor above, and the spaces thus plunge back and forth like the pistons in an engine.

These radial motions in towards the centre and out again are the primary device of the building and are loosely associated with a trend in the 2000s for cantilevered, 'hovering' building elements of which the Dutch MVRDV has been a strong exponent. It is thus the relief, not the circle as such, that restrains the fleeting character of the neighbourhood. Each individual student flat is emphasized in the facade. The 360 rooms have been placed on the outward-facing side; it is from there that the individual resident is in visual contact with the surrounding world. It is from there one comes in and from there one must one day depart again. Inward towards the courtyard lie only communal functions, such as kitchens and TV rooms. Here there are even larger bays which with up to eight metres of cantilevering are drawn out and pushed into even more intense motion. They serve as kitchens and balconies that both contain and express the force and intensity of the community.

The crucial point for the residents' experience of living in the hall of residence is that no one has a room down at the end far from the communality of the kitchen. Everywhere the residents are equally close, and one engages or disengages with the collectivity by crossing the corridor.

The variation in the building feels strong, but constructionally there are many repetitions, and prefabricated elements have been used for the concrete skeleton, which is visible from the inside. The skin consists of oak and tombac, an alloy of copper and zinc which hardly oxidizes but patinates to a brown colour. The materials give the building a dark, warm tone that unifies the many projections.

Constructionally it is like a round woodpile, but programmatically it is like a cone where the centre of the collectivity provides the nutrients with which the seeds are sent out into the world.

The floors with rooms hover over a tall, transparent and undercut base where one finds many of the hall of residence's collective functions, such as meeting and study rooms, administration, workshops, cycle racks and a laundry. These are functions which in halls of residence are often hidden away in basement rooms that are experienced as insecure and murky. Here they are elevated into daylight and out on to the panopticon that is the building.

The panopticon is a building type that the moral philosopher Jeremy Bentham described in 1791: a round and well-lit building with a darkened watchtower in the middle. The consciousness that one could never know when one was being monitored out on the ring was meant to have a disciplining effect on the inmates. The model was a universal solution, as Bentham pointed out, and could be used for everything from prisons to schools and mental hospitals. In the Tietgen Hall of Residence there is no tower in the middle and no hidden watchmen, but there is the gaze of the other student residents across the courtyard – something that in our age also has a socializing effect, for you can always see where the party is.

Tietgen Hall of Residence

Address:
Rued Langgårdsvej 10-18, Copenhagen S

Area:
26,500 m², 21,900 m² of which above ground

Number of apartments: 360

Client:
Tietgen Hall of Residence Foundation and Nordea-fonden

Client's consultants:
Niras A/S, Hasløv & Kjærsgaard and Freja Ejendomme

Engineering: COWI A/S

Landscape architects:
Marianne Levinsen A/S
and Henrik Jørgensen A/S

Artistic consultants:
Aggebo & Henriksen

Dates:
First Prize in project competition 2002
Built in 2003-06

Awards:
Diploma of Foreningen til Hovedstadens. Forskønnelse, 2005
Træprisen 2006
Copenhagen City Council, 2006
Copenhagen Cultural Foundation, 2006
Træprisen, 2006
RIBA European Award 2007
Concrete Element Prize 2007
The Aid Forum Award/Best Nordic Interior 2007

Pragmatic regionalism

The importance of the architecture of the Tietgen Hall of Residence to the residents, to the neighbourhood Ørestad North, to the branding of Copenhagen as an internationally attractive university city and an architectural tourist attraction can hardly be overestimated. The image of the round building with its large bays – often seen in Jens Lindhe's picture taken from the courtyard shortly after the inauguration – has spread widely and is often part of narratives about the new 'funky' Copenhagen.

And indeed they are a strong feature of the building, but in terms of social function this is due to nothing but generosity towards the residents. For passers-by the dense atmosphere of the building is of a more aesthetic character. Depending on one's broad-mindedness one is pleased on behalf of the students or a little envious of them, but it is not a building that leaves you unmoved. The building rests in itself with great authority, and the constructional clarity and high finish mean that its staggered modules are not experienced as a random postulate. You believe that it is a house that delivers the student adventure promised by the cantilevered blocks with great aplomb.

Phenomenologically it is a giant tree stump, anchoring a fleeting urban space, and offers a glimpse of what regionalism can be today in a place that appears globalized, without a history. It is not concerned with the evocation of other styles or building customs but with fulfilling a specific social function with an approach that gives the meagre context of the place much-needed weight. In some ways it is Lundgaard & Tranberg's most succinct building, because the approach is so simple, robust and uncompromising. It has been given its form by the wish to have this radial reciprocity with the surroundings which, like pistons in an urban engine, works for and at the place. It is here too that the firm comes closest to the Dutch pragmatism which in those years exerted such a significant influence on Danish architecture through a new generation of architects with Bjarke Ingels's drawing offices Plot and BIG and Dan Stubbergaard's COBE as the prime examples. With its diagram-clear divisions the building recalls that more conceptual and sometimes bragging architecture, but the proportioning and the consistent choices of materials outweigh the intensely baroque features. Other materials and other colours might easily have made the building unbearably self-assertive.

But although the architecture appears visually generous, the functions are exclusively for the residents. It does not open up its grounds to passers-by. No seating, kiosk or other functions open the building up to the outside. The landscaping attempts to mediate between the meadow and river-like landscape on one side of the building and the promenade with its city canal on the other. It does not have a strength to match that of the building. In fact as a rule there is free access to the courtyard, but through large lattice gates that you only open if you know that you can and feel invited to.

Knotty. The deep relief and the round basic form break with Ørestad's long straight lines and smooth facades. Seen here from Emil Holms Kanal.

Expressive. The relief becomes even stronger and deeper when you enter the courtyard. The facade expresses individuality, the courtyard collectivity.

Outside spaces. You can get outside the hall of residence on large communal balconies, the balconies of the rooms and on the stairwell between the five sections of the building, where wisteria grows.

Factory. Exposed structures give the communal spaces of the hall of residence a bold industrial atmosphere that is underscored by the robust lamps and the few but bright colours as in the kitchen chairs and the letterbox hatches.

Furnished. The student rooms are furnished with a large multifunctional feature in birch veneer. The semicircle contains a cabinet shower.

Urban. With 360 students the hall of residence is an entire small village. In the evening across the courtyard it is as if the veil of the facade has been dropped and you feel one another's lives.

The Playhouse and Kvæsthus Pier

Architecture is applied sociology, says partner Peter Thorsen. None of the buildings of the drawing office shows more clearly what he means by this than the new Playhouse of the Royal Danish Theatre. As one of the culture palaces of the 2000s it is, perhaps surprisingly, not terribly spectacular. Despite the large and highly impressive glass-covered top storey, which projects out over a wooden promenade with a filigree of window frames and ventilating swivel windows, it is visually a rather subdued building. With its resemblance to the warehouses of the harbour it is first and foremost a massive lump lying outermost on the edge of the quay. But its appearance is less about how it looks than about what it offers: how it guides people into and around it, how it gets people to meet in various ways and how it involves and activates the whole harbour space as a framework for those meetings.

The weight of the buildings matches that of the long pier Kvæsthusbroen, which ends in a ramp down in the water. Together the two form a dynamic span in the harbour space in an intricate play of darkness and light, weight and lightness, mass and surface. But socially too there is a great difference between the two ends of the composition. While one creates an intense setting for city life, theatrical art and human togetherness, the other is a place where you go out and can be alone with the water, the harbour and the sky. This end is not part of the intense, event-worshipping city life where every day is a party or a visit to the café. It is a place where you can take a break from exactly that. This very freedom from programming has made the urban space of the pier incredibly popular, and it is occupied by all sorts of activities from company team building and yoga sessions to sunbathing.

'The population is gasping for examples of good architecture. The fantastic, the innovative, the surprising, the unimaginable. Until it is there,' Boje Lundgaard said to the newspaper *Politiken* in 2002 when the firm's proposal was revealed as the winner of the open international competition ahead of 330 other proposals.

The Opera's opposite number

At that time the building of the Opera designed by Henning Larsen Architects diagonally opposite was already well in hand. And the two new departments of the Royal Danish Theatre with their almost identical functions resemble each other superficially. They are both oriented with audience areas out towards the water and have secondary facades on the other sides, marked by a more closed, solid building massif. Frontally they have a glass-covered foyer beneath a strikingly projecting roof surface and are crowned at the top by a smaller, almost cubic stage tower.

All the same they are as day and night. The relationship of the Opera to its close surroundings is almost non-existent; it is oriented exclusively towards the water surface, Frederiksstad and the royal palace of Amalienborg on the other side of the water. The shipowner Mærsk McKinney-Møller, the client for the Opera, imagined it as a sculpture on a surface and wanted it to stand free in the fairway, like a ship at sea, as a magnificent gift to the city and the Danish people, and not least to the Queen, who resides just opposite. It was thus placed as the endpoint of an axis that goes from Frederiks Kirke (the 'Marble Church') through the Amalienborg palace square and as in Nicolai Eigtved's plan for Frederiksstad from 1749 was conceived as open to the rising sun in the east. The Opera strikingly breaks with the scale of the fine buildings behind; it is strictly symmetrical in structure, its materials are light in colour and its design stylized, underscored most strongly in its large roof projection. This makes the body language of the Opera stiff-necked, one-sidedly oriented towards royalty with a corresponding blindness to its close surroundings, the adjacent islets which lie as two urban deserts – one a lawn, the other a parking lot. The building was designed to be surrounded by lower buildings, but that possibility has not yet been exploited by the owner, the A.P. Møller Foundation.

By contrast the Playhouse enters at all levels into a close, inviting and more relaxed interplay with its place. First and foremost it steps aside for the less grand axis of the square Sankt Annæ Plads, which demarcates Frederiksstad to the south. It was inherent in the international competition for the Playhouse that it could be placed either to the right or left of Sankt Annæ Plads, which in reality is a two-way street with a small park in the middle.

To make it a part of the row of buildings on Kvæsthusgade the drawing office placed the Playhouse to the right in front of Kvæsthuset, Copenhagen's first hospital, which has given its name to both the street and the pier, which in accordance with the old terminology is still called a bridge ('bro'). Today the old hospital building houses the Danish Nursing Council, and in order to emphasize that the Playhouse was just another building in the row, both facade and roof height were allowed to follow the lines of the building, which thus, admittedly, lost its view of the water.

The Playhouse lies here on the border between two city districts, each with its own strong identity – the old fishermen's and amusement neighbourhood Nyhavn and the aristocratic Frederiksstad. That the roof height is flush with the old hospital building's, however, is only a minor element that disappears visually given the very different expressions of the two buildings. The Playhouse appears to be stacked and composed of very large elements with a massive block at the bottom and a projecting glass disc above, held in place at the top by the copper block of the stage tower. These are large and decidedly horizontal features, unlike the vertically oriented and more etched facade of the Kvæsthus building.

In Kvæsthusgade it inserts itself simply as part of the ribbon development of the street. It is experienced clearly as the back of the building; this is where the loading area for the stage sets is, and this is where the various theatrical staff have their entrance. But both the fine facing and the large window openings into the theatre's workshop soften the meeting of the mass with the street. The fine masonry with its low, deep window openings is a polite but firm marking of the private zone of the building. You experience it as a workplace. But you are invited to look in as you pass by. As a pedestrian in Kvæsthusgade you feel neither invited in nor entirely shut out.

Social attraction

Invited is certainly how you feel at the front. Here a space has been created that is so pleasant that it encourages people to make their way around the building and stay a while inside or on the wooden deck in front.

The public arrives at the theatre at the front. The building is so deep that it interrupts the course of the harbour promenade and projects out over the edge of the quayside. The interrupted promenade is extended here by a soft deck of oak planks, and this is one of the true strokes of genius in the building. Unlike Vilhelm Dahlerup's tall staircase which separated the art from the street and everyday life and attuned the mind to an elevating experience on the Old Stage, here your progress is horizontal. True, the deck is raised a little over the quayside and lands on it by way of long ramps. But it gives the sensation of walking out on a platform borne by bandy legs, which in a quite different but no less effective way than the stairway up to the Old Stage attunes the public to the approaching encounter with art in the Playhouse. The oak feels warm and soft; it has a different sound from the hard ground of the quay, and you hear the water splashing against its legs and can glimpse it gleaming through the cracks. Up on the deck you have quite another sensory contact with the watery element than on the hard quayside, and the contrast can remind you that the quay was originally not intended for human traffic but for the servicing of big ships.

In good weather the wooden deck urges you to take a seat. Either on one of the café chairs or directly on the deck. But it is not just a large patio which functions at the same time as a continuation of the harbour promenade, where pedestrians and cycles flow in and out among one another. The depth of the deck leaves plenty of room for different speeds at the same time, and incisions create pockets on the pier where you can sit quietly and dangle your feet out over the water without feeling that you are sitting in the middle of a cycle path.

The raised wooden deck has no protective wall other than a very low rim because it is regarded as part of the quayside, which has historically never been fenced off. It is not only for people with business in the theatre, and it has become a popular meeting place at the harbour. With the slight rise of the ramp, the wood and the water beneath your feet, you feel here that you are stepping into a different zone. Not so much an elevated place as a place where you can lower your speed a little and breathe a little deeper.

Like the stairway to the Old Stage, the wooden deck offers a rite of passage that fine-tunes the mind and leads you from the everyday into the theatre. It is only the first of several zones you have to pass through before you reach the anticipated performances in the heart of the building.

The theatre foyer is also a public space, open in the daytime hours. The light is perceptibly dimmed when you come into the foyer. Above, the large glass disc projects out with a black ceiling and hanging balconies. The dark brick of the facade has accompanied you in and forms a back wall in the foyer. Balconies in black steel hang down from the ceiling, and the floor surface consists of dark cross-cut timbers. Here you are in an intermediate zone where you are protected from wind and weather, clearly not quite inside the theatre yet but sill in a continuing multifunctional space with a restaurant, cloakroom and a mobile stage where various cultural events take place. The dark frames around the glass wall mean that reflexes are minimized and the glass, which has less iron in it than normal, is as transparent as possible. The dimmed lighting is created by a wealth of suspended and screened-off light conduits, a starry shower of lianas – or black spaghetti, if you like, where the actual light source is hidden so it does not reflect in the glass. This means that the glass surface is not covered with reflexes, that in daylight you can look into the foyer and in the evening you can experience the harbour space becoming the true background of the foyer.

Unfortunately the low light intensity in the foyer also bothers some people. You do not only go to the theatre to experience the harbour, the architecture and the acting; you also go to see one another and be seen. A theatre audience after all acts out its own little play.

The last zone that separates the city and its everyday life from the world of the play is the stairway that leads up to the balconies. From there you enter the masonry massif, the auditorium, the theatre itself, where the performance awaits you.

The Grotto

While the approach to the theatre and the relationship with the surrounding world is much more modern and all-embracing, the actual core of the theatre is as classic as can be imagined. The drawing office worked with several models for a theatre interior in the Large Stage but ended up with the most classic form – the so-called proscenium model.

The audience area describes a semicircle protruding from the front of the stage and feels very intimate despite the fact that there are 650 seats. The stage front draws a line that separates the audience from the performers, and although this is not visible, it runs exactly where the quay meets the water. This is where the performing artist is put to the test facing the sea of the audience.

The solid nature of the facade has been drawn into this beating heart of the theatre, where it has a different, cave-like character. The hall is lined with the same bricks as the facade but in this case in an intensely rugged bonding that breaks up the sound waves and creates the acoustics of the hall. With a reverberation time of exactly one second, it is ideal for spoken-word drama and adds to the intimate atmosphere of the hall.

The rugged bonding of the brickwork is further dramatized by being illuminated from below, and together with the red upholstery of the seats it gives the space an atmosphere of warmth and closeness. Like the gold and stucco decoration of the Old Stage, the walls here become stage sets for the small drama it already is for people to take their seats. The dark brick-clad grotto supports the energy and intimacy with its encapsulation of the audience area. Finding the right enveloping form was one of the things the drawing office worked most with in the project:

'It takes its inspiration from the old Italian box theatres, the classic theatres and of course from Shakespeare's round theatre. It is very intriguing that when you think you have to create a revolutionary theatre, you end up with the proscenium theatre, which is the place that was established when the theatre moved indoors and separated play and audience with a stage front,' says Lene Tranberg.

'But the elements play together inasmuch as we sit together in an arc. We are not in the cinema, in a line, we are together in this special moment when audience and actors are close. This way we get 650 people to feel that they are almost sitting at the feet of the actors – or as a corollary, that the actors are truly close to their audience. You feel the importance of the closeness of those performing to those who are to absorb the experience.'

The theatre also has its Small Stage, which is a 'black box' room with seating for 100 spectators, and a Gate Stage where the acting is oriented out of the building and the audience gathers on the square Ofelia Plads, as the theatre calls the city space on Kvæsthus Pier.

Breaking down hierarchies

So not only people flow around and through the playhouse; the acting also comes out of the building and flows into the foyer, out on to the deck or the Kvæsthus Pier, where several options for live performance are on hand. A small stage is built into one of the Kvæsthus Pier's small, tombac-clad service buildings, and the service towers with sound and lighting mean that concerts or drama can be performed directly on the surface of the Kvæsthus Pier. The horizontal orientation softens the boundary between art and the everyday. By simply moving past the building you risk becoming a more or less voluntary audience to a play.

It is a feature of the time that cultural institutions step down this way from their pedestals, that they lie down flat on the ground and invite people in, signalling that going to the theatre is no longer a pursuit of the elite.

But the breakdown of the hierarchy of art has not only affected the relations between art and the public; it has also affected the staff of the theatre in the service areas behind and above the stage where the public has no access:

'It's a quite different situation. Taking its cue from the Old Stage's super-hierarchical, labyrinthine structure, we could see that there was a certain resistance in the collaboration in the workplace. The divisions between primadonnas and waterboys were too rigid. A modern theatre must also reflect the time it lives in, so we omitted these divisions. Of course one has one's function and one's delimited sphere, but we put them all under one and the same roof, and you get fluid transitions,' says Lene Tranberg.

Up here behind the green glass the staff have their workplace at a level dominated by very strong, exposed lattice girders that bear up the storey in its low suspension above the foyer. At the very front above the wooden deck lie the staff canteen and meeting place. The best position and view are not reserved for the director or the interns but is the place where everyone from cleaning staff to star actors comes.

The soul of the brickwork

The massive character of the building plays against the weight of the traditional warehouses of the harbour and the Opera opposite, but when you get close to the Playhouse, its long, flat, hand-crafted bricks go down and take hold on a very small scale and in fact are experienced in richer detail than the actual plastered facades of Frederiksstad's haute-bourgeois mansions with their fine facade reliefs.

The bricks were made in collaboration with the firm Petersen Tegl and are a darker development of a brick that Peter Zumthor

The Kvæsthus Project

Address:
Sankt Annæ Plads 36, Copenhagen K

The Playhouse

Area:
21,000 m²

Client:
The Royal Danish Theatre / The Ministry of Culture

Client's consultants:
Moe & Brødgaard A/S and Erik Møllers tegnestue

Engineering:
COWI A/S

Landscaping:
Lundgaard & Tranberg Arkitekter

Acoustics:
Gade & Mortensen A/S

Lighting design:
Jesper Kongshaug

Artistic consultants:
Finn Reinbothe, John Kørner and Peter Holst Henckel

Graphics:
Aggebo & Henriksen

Dates:
First Prize in open international competition, 2002
Built in 2004-07

Awards:
Diploma from Foreningen til Hovedstadens Forskønnelse, 2007
The Danish Lighting Prize, 2008
RIBA European Award 2008
Nordic Lighting Prize 2008
Copenhagen City Council, 2008
Sustainable Concrete Prize, 2009

Kvæsthus Pier

Area:
Parking complex: 17,800 m²,
500 parking places
Urban space 16,000 m²

Client:
Kvæsthusselskabet A/S

Engineering:
COWI A/S

Traffic consultant:
Viatrafik

Landscaping:
Lundgaard & Tranberg Arkitekter
and Julie Kierkegaard

Artistic consultant:
Finn Reinbothe

Dates:
Built: 2013-16

has produced in a lighter version for his museum Kolumba in Cologne, from which the brick has taken its name. The Kolumba brick is just four centimetres in height but half a metre long (!), hand-crafted and fired at varying temperatures, which give it rich variation in colour and form. No two bricks are identical; many curve slightly and the surfaces of the Playhouse bricks seem to shimmer in dark brown shades, with elements of red, blue and yellow colours and with white flecks.

The material and its aesthetic qualities are crucial to the experience of the building's atmosphere, which is at once everyday and sophisticated. Retiring, mature and rich. It is, as the historian of ideas Carsten Thau points out in the book *Art of Many,* indicative of a particularly Danish regionalism that takes its point of departure in P.V. Jensen Klint's sober yet also ecstatic use of brick as both a constructional and decorative element in the Grundtvig Church and which Kay Fisker perpetuated in his Functionalist tradition, which in his work with C.F. Møller reached its high point in Aarhus University. These were ways of making the brick express a national building style which for P.V. Jensen Klint contrasted with the far more internationally influenced, decorative and materially varied works such as Martin Nyrop's City Hall in Copenhagen or Anton Rosen's Palace Hotel.

The consistent attitude to the material expresses a frugality which at the same time becomes a balancing act in craftsmanship when the bricks are allowed to bear the whole expression of a building. The material, which can be handled by a single person and thus requires no machinery, is a nod to the medieval crafts and infuses the project with a spirit that is otherwise felt to have been lost in modern pre-cast construction. Some may think it has been cultivated to excess in the Playhouse, where the bricks are handmade, fired at a variety of temperatures and pressed to become as expressive as possible, while at the same time there is the restrained, economical attitude that only one material must bear and express the whole soul of the building. It is in the cultivation of the material as the bearer of ideologies such as honesty and sincerity that regionalism is said to live on in Lundgaard & Tranberg's architecture, but it would be wrong to take this as indicative of a characteristically Nordic or Danish architecture. The bricks may have been fired by Danish craftsmen in South Jutland, but the special clay is English, and the care to ensure that a single material can form the whole expression of a building is something they share, for example, with like-minded Swiss drawing offices like Peter Zumthor and Herzog & de Meuron.

Background. The Playhouse is a mass and a boulder which, despite its prominent position and fine details, makes no effort to impress unnecessarily.

Balancing act. The huge projection with heavy lattice girders on the service storey hangs over the foyer, which is simply a light framing of part of the harbour space.

Transparency. The floor, ceiling and walls of the foyer are dark, so the experience of the harbour space is the true motif.

Det Kongelige Teater

uespil
nuset

Air. In quiet architecture the detailing is important. This is where the atmosphere lowers or increases its intensity.

Alternations. Like the brick, the building is dominated by horizontal lines, while cut-outs in the ceiling and balconies give it airiness and views between up and down.

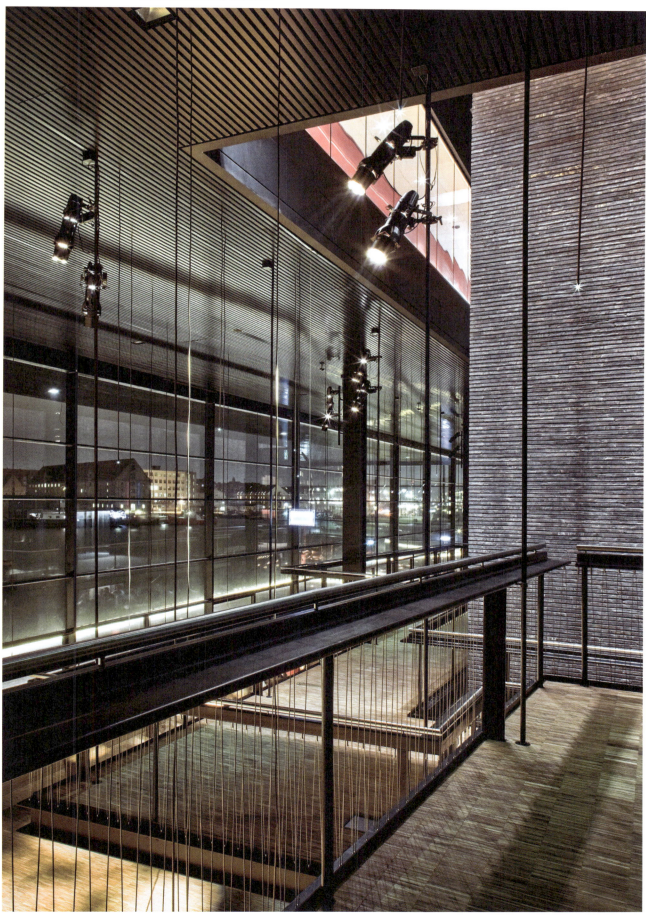

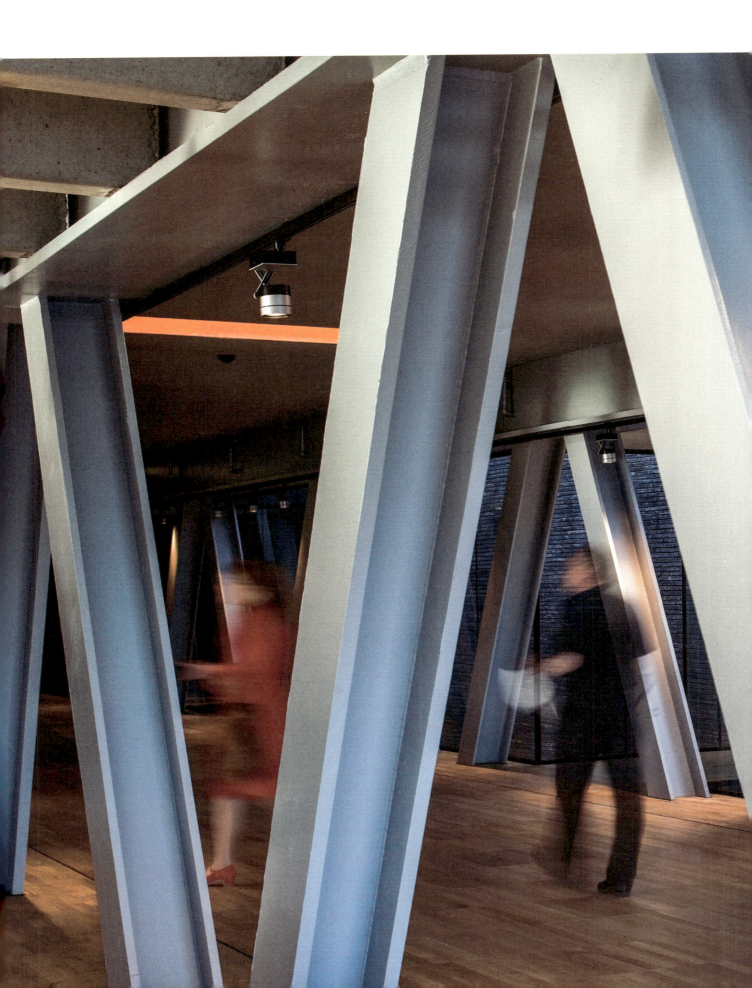

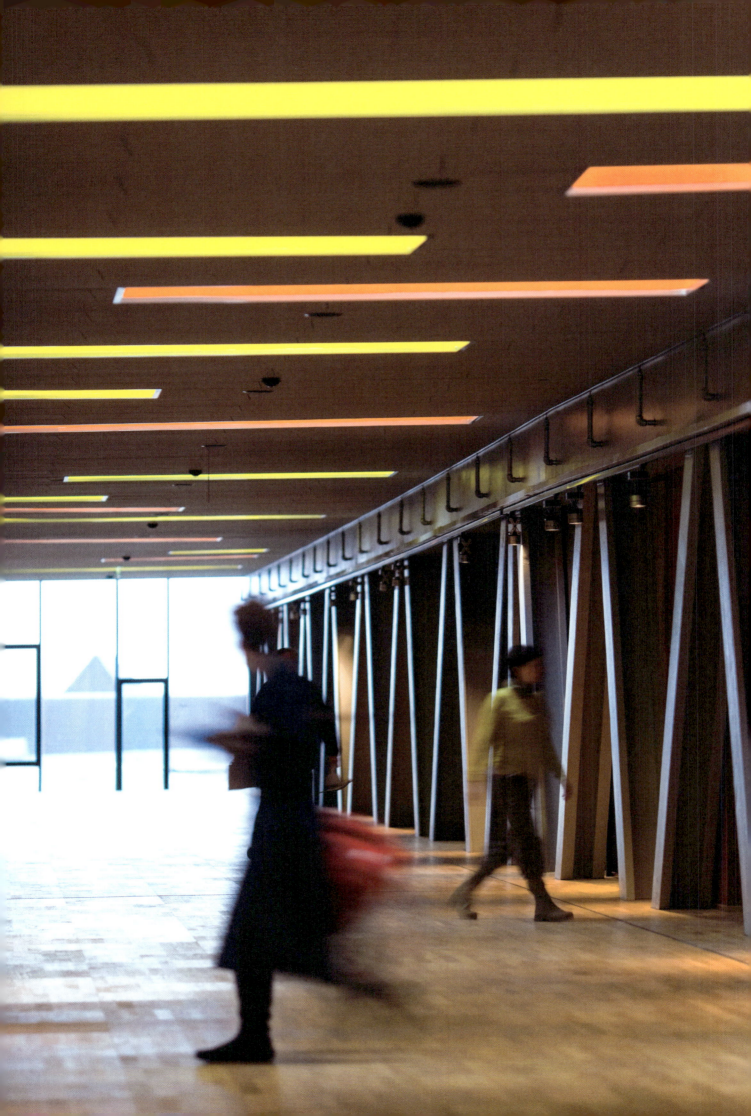

Rigging loft. The lattice girders of the service storey are exposed and function as partitions. In the tower too the stage technology is suspended in lattice constructions.

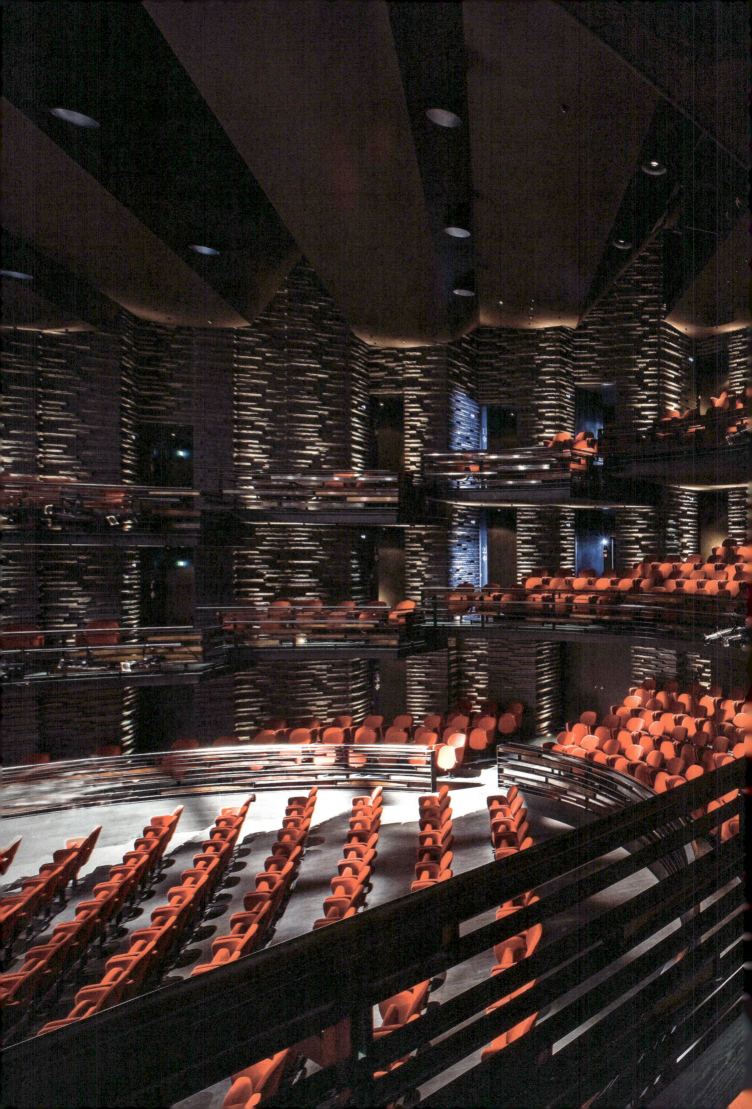

Brittle. The dark concrete surface of the pier is surrounded by rusted corten steel. Handmade lateral grooves give the large surfaces a human scale and a rich finish.

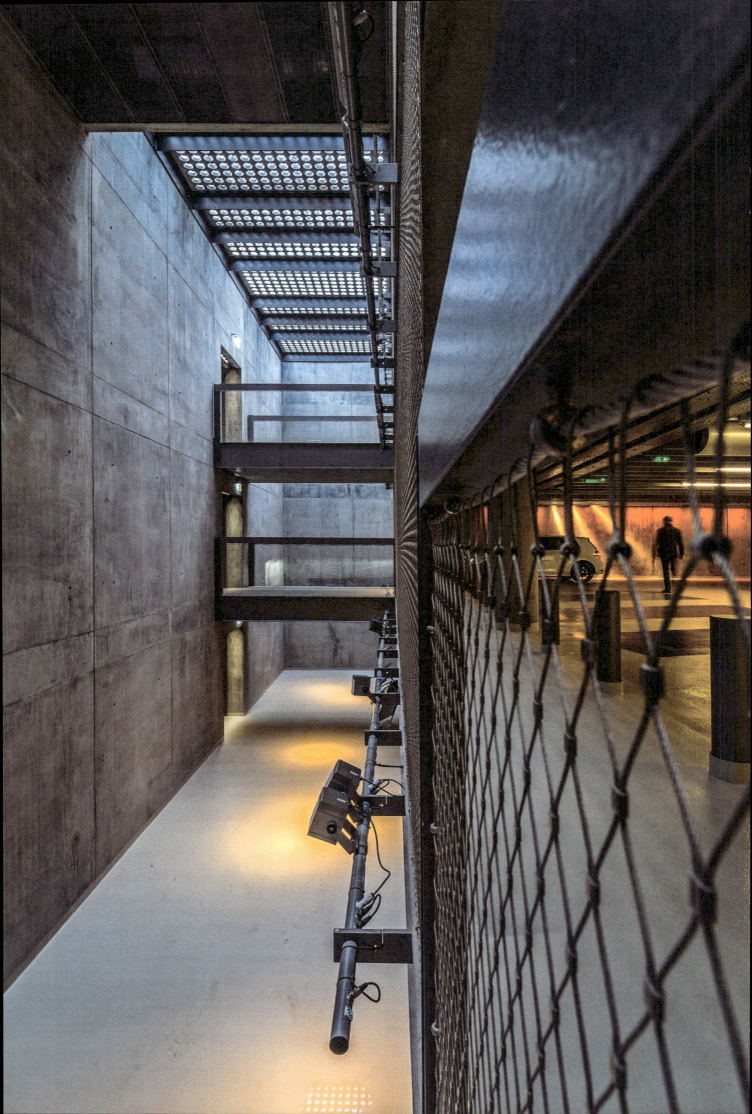

Emphasis. In the 320-metre-long, 40-metre-wide pier there are three parking storeys with room for 500 cars. Artificial lighting warms the space.

Surroundings. The long descent of the pier down to the water surface directs the attention to the harbour, the city and the sky.

About the drawing office

The architectural decision that leads to the design of a project is not something that arises in a moment of clear-sightedness as a quick sketch from a master's hand on a table napkin or as the idea of a single individual. The hierarchy of Lundgaard & Tranberg Arkitekter's drawing office is rather flat – like Denmark, you could say. All trainees are given responsibility from the first day, and the recently graduated can immediately become part of a team with responsibility for implementing a construction project. This broad delegation of responsibility is only possible because all the partners get involved in all the jobs and stand ready with their support and experience.

In 'flat' organizations like the dysfunctional firm that Lars von Trier caricatures in his film comedy *The Boss of it All*, the power is always hard to pinpoint, and it takes the right chemistry to fit into an invisible hierarchy that is based on trust. Although as a new member of staff at Lundgaard & Tranberg Arkitekter you can have great influence from day one if you have something to offer, you cannot just charge off and take the projects wherever you want. You have to convince the group that it is the right thing to do.

The flat structure is a challenge when the drawing office grows. For if all the partners are to be involved in all the projects, there is a limit to how many jobs they can manage. In 2016 they had a number of major projects and have now grown to a staff of seventy-five. In the Danish context that is considered a medium-large drawing office, but it has never in itself been an ambition for them to be big – only to keep control of the finances and the building techniques, so they maintain stability and the ability to realize the architectural visions.

The partner group therefore represents not only architectural expertise but also finances and building technology. Today it consists of the architects Lene Tranberg, Erik Frandsen, Henrik Schmidt, Nicolai Richter-Friis, the building designer Philip Heiberg, managing director and architect Peter Thorsen and the business economist Trine Troelsen. But it is Lene Tranberg who, as founding partner, is singled out again and again in the press, and it is she who has been awarded the Academy's highest distinction, the C.F. Hansen Medal. Nevertheless, on all possible occasions she points out that architecture is never a solo feat, that she could do nothing alone, that it is the whole team that stands behind the work every time and that the creative process really functions in the collectivity with the very open tone of the firm.

The aim for the management of the firm is not that the individual should make the whole impact; on the contrary, it is to step back and make its role superfluous. Because the true aim is the vibrant interplay of everyone's best abilities.

Everyone can contribute at any time, and they are not afraid to criticize, shut

131

down a project and start from scratch if that is what feels right. This may sound like a crazy waste of time, but it is a necessary detour you may have to take in a creative process and is a responsibility to the client, the job and the future which the partners take very seriously. 'Enthusiasm and doubt are our most important tools,' says Peter Thorsen. Architecture is about creating values that are not only measured in dollars and cents but are also about people's well-being in their homes, their workplaces, in urban spaces and in cities. They simply consider architecture far too serious to deliver something that is only 'good enough'.

For example, Erik Frandsen was able with a casual remark to change the design of the Museum of Danish Resistance. For a long time a working group at the drawing office had tried out various pavilions on the competition site. Erik Frandsen came by, looked at the scene and quickly remarked that the structures would be too expensive. But then he said that they really shouldn't build anything in front of the Citadel, the old city fortress. That would be a shame for the place. That remark prompted the drawing office to investigate the idea of going underground, so the Danish resistance would be just as hidden as it was during the war, and instead leaving the surface above without new buildings, as a place where openness could pay homage to freedom.

The dialectic between above and below, free and hidden turned out to be the basis of the proposal they pursued further and with which they later won the competition. That this was the fifth time the drawing office went wholly or partly underground in the creation of a museum building was more or less a coincidence. Each time it has been the situation and the surroundings that have determined what seemed to be the right thing to do, that made the project 'vibrate'. Just as humility is a characteristic of Lene Tranberg's way of managing her position as founder of the firm, it is an approach the drawing office likes to take in its architecture. They are quite willing to step aside to let other qualities of a place than those of their own building take the foreground.

The building then becomes a setting for the evocation of a larger context. This happened for example when in the work with the Playhouse they moved it from a siting at the end of the square Sankt Annæ Plads and instead pushed it out to the side, so that it continued flush with the row of houses and heights of the roofs on Sankt Annæ Plads. Even with as prominent a cultural institution with such a massive presence as the Playhouse of the Royal Danish Theatre, they have stepped aside out of respect for the surroundings.

Something similar could be noted when they later developed Kvæsthus Pier as a parking complex and urban space. The parking was taken underground, and the pier was kept free of programming and development, apart from the row of small service pavilions along the Kvæsthus moat, which hints at a division of the space in syncopated rhythms. The approach has provided a water surface untroubled by disturbing buildings. It is courageous to say that there should be nothing there. *Horror vacui*, the fear of the empty space, is usually a strong force in the planning of city space, but the drawing office has seen that, simply with the finely finished surface that disappears down into the water, they have done enough. Instead of a feature that unnecessarily draws attention to itself, it becomes a platform for experiencing the whole harbour space. By holding back they have grasped something bigger.

Humility towards the surroundings can thus be a way of evoking the spirit of the place. Constructing a grand, blustering building is by no means as courageous as daring to leave well alone. And perhaps some of the firm's most impressive feats lie in its ability to convince their clients that humility can be the right solution.

History of the drawing office

In 1975 Boje Lundgaard founded a drawing office with his then wife, Bente Aude. Along with the landscape architect Svend Kierkegaard they were commissioned to design the private project Sjølund in Hellebæk in 1977-79. This is a dense, low linked-housing project with high recreative qualities in close harmony with the landscape. The inspiration from Jørn Utzon's Kingo Houses and the Fredensborg Houses is clear. Sjølund's seventy-four homes are spatially varied into nineteen types but have a uniform character, built exclusively in yellow brick, black-painted wood and yellow tile and either oriented around a lake, out towards a forest or towards the nearby coast. There is a harmony with nature in the project but also a sober simplicity in its pre-industrial materials.

The focus on the encounter of the project with the character of the terrain became even clearer in 1982 when the firm won the contract for the Trapholt Art Museum, which follows a slope down towards Kolding Fjord. Trapholt is a structuralist project with galleries that accompany one another along a passage. But it is a soft, musical structure that listens and responds to the place. When the floor descends, the ceiling height rises. The topography pushes at the structure; it allows itself to be influenced. In one place the space descends slightly, in another it does not reach that far and gets a little light from the sky instead, and in the next place it goes out and takes in the view. Variation in the ways of drawing the light in lets the motion through the museum breathe. This is not just repetition after repetition of identical spatialities, normally a characteristic of Structuralism.

Boje Lundgaard taught at the Royal Academy of Fine Arts, and one of his students was Lene Tranberg. After Boje had divorced and Lene Tranberg had graduated from the Academy in 1984, the two became partners privately and professionally.

This also became the true start of the drawing office Lundgaard & Tranberg. They won the competition for Blangstedgård near Odense, an experimental 'new town' project where many of the new drawing offices of the time had the opportunity to try their hand at housing construction. The plan here was that the houses were to lie like notes in sheet music or apples on a tree and would create a close relationship between landscape and housing. There were experiments with postmodernism, neoclassicism and a regionalism of an idyllic-romantic character which the drawing office further unfolded in the project Allerød Have with allusions to English housing projects. In this linked-housing project, too, great variation in the house types was evident in the facades.

In subsequent years, before projects in the capital began, they created several such housing projects on open ground as well as kindergartens and industrial complexes. The industrial complexes, especially the power and district heating plants in Horsens, Faaborg and Svendborg, were expressed in basic geometrical forms which, especially in Faaborg, had allusions to the adventurous classical forms of the Neoclassicist Étienne-Louis Boullée.

But two things in particular preoccupied the drawing office: the environment and construction design. After the industrialization of construction, architecture had become a kind of curating of already-designed products. You looked up the manufacturer's catalogues of doors and windows and put them together as well as you could. If you wanted to create a more effective project you had to start by designing the processes and the products in the construction sector. The partner Filip Heiberg, who is a construction designer and has been with the firm almost from the start, points out that it was the commission for the Helsingør Sewage Disposal Plant in those years in particular that changed the firm's attitude as to how far they could go as architects and take responsibility for more parts of the design process. With large technical plants the architecture only represents a very small part of the price, so there is slightly more scope than in the ordinary housing projects, where you have to count every penny. Then they discovered that you could collaborate with the manufacturers to design your own windows and even end up doing it for the same prices as the standard products.

In 1996 in Ballerup, along with the Danish Institute of Construction Research, they built a high-insulation low-energy glass house. This was a continuation of some of the firm's earlier investigations of how, with large glass areas, one could passively store solar heat in a massive construction, as in a house with solid walls, but at the same time have the advantage offered by the glass – a high level of daylight. The angular, minimalistic box functioned at first as a trial home and later as a communal building for the surrounding projects. The experience from this project led to later works dominated by exterior walls with glass, such as the Danish Industry Hall of Residence in Nørrebro in Copenhagen, The Wedge in Frederiksberg and to some extent the Villa in Hellerup for Birgit Lyngbye Pedersen.

Privately Boje Lundgaard and Lene Tranberg broke up in 1994 after twelve years of living together and started new families that were to maintain close contacts with one another. Professionally they continued their partnership managing the drawing office until Boje's sudden death from a heart attack at the age of just sixty in 2004. Lene Tranberg then changed the management structure to a broad partnership, which remains unchanged today except for the departure of the architect Kenneth Warnke in 2012.

Important projects from this period to today are presented in this book. But many others could have been included and studied in more depth: housing projects like Fyrtårnet (The Lighthouse) and Havneholmen, university buildings such as the Copenhagen Plant Science Centre at Copenhagen University and Niagara in Malmö, cultural buildings such as the Castle Museum in Vordingborg and Kannikegården, the Moravian Brethren's building in Ribe. But it has not been the intention to write an exhaustive description of the works, only to pick out a number of important examples of their production, which by no means appears to be a closed chapter.

Projects on the drawing board include contributions to exclusive international competitions: a new school for Ørestad, a Danish Museum of Natural History and a large-scale urban development project between Copenhagen Central Station and SEB with homes, businesses and new city spaces on the site of the old Post Office Terminal.

Sorø Art Museum

The annexe to the Sorø Art Museum builds on a narrative about the structure of the town. It is a smallish project with a tight budget, which nevertheless produces a distinctive atmosphere with its consistency and inventive use of materials. The facade and roof cladding could almost be seen as a reinvention of brick and tile, but it is the cohesion with the town, its new connections and its great spatial dynamism that make it a small masterpiece.

The Sorø Art Museum has a fine collection of Danish art and Russian icons from 1500 to today and was originally accommodated in a town house on Storgade. The building is from 1832 and served as the home of the estate manager at Sorø Academy until the fine rooms were furnished in 1943 as the town's art museum.

For many years there was a dream of building a new museum by the lake outside the town, where there would be room for the growing collection and better visitors' facilities. A competition was held for the project, which Lundgaard & Tranberg Arkitekter won. But fortunately for the cultural life of the historic core of Sorø, the project could not raise the funding, and in the end a new competition was held for an extension of the museum on the existing site. This competition too was won by Lundgaard & Tranberg with a project that took its cue from the structure of the old town.

Several of Sorø's houses have a courtyard structure with front and back buildings, so it seemed logical also to complete the museum site in this way. The extension has been conceived and constructed as a back building, a wing that reflects the main building across the courtyard and connects the two through a lower intermediate building. The extension, like a barn on a farm, has fewer but larger openings and is less detailed than the front building. But even with this subordinate role it has been possible to give it a striking character with no less integrity than the main building.

A reinvention of brick shingle

The facade of the earlier estate manager's lodge out to the main street has so-called Hamburg jointing, where the mortar joints protrude in relief and seem to stand and shimmer between the dark bricks. The front building was to remain the main constructional motif of the museum, and the drawing office wanted the facade of the extension to have a similar effect but something which at the same time was true to the technology of its time. It was after all the distinctive feature of the museum to have special masonry.

The solution was to 're-invent' shingles and, instead of laying the fired clay as bricks, to hang it up as if it were light facade cladding. The extension was constructed like a barn with a steel skeleton, over which the facade was drawn like a screen. It is built up of an unusually beautiful *shingle tile* laid lap-jointed which the drawing office developed along with Petersen Tegl. The clay is fired in varied hues of the type known from their collaboration on Kolumba bricks for the Playhouse. In this case it is just a thin pantile that is fixed to both roof and facade without mortar. The facade is therefore maintenance-free and without the unsightly elastic expansion joints that are necessary so brick sidings do not crack.

As in the Playhouse and in the housing project Charlottehaven in Østerbro from 2001, the brick is saturated from the start. It does not stand fresh as is normal practice for newly fired factory bricks, which are not yet patinated by wind, weather and dirt.

The uniform facing gives the building a monolithic character. Although it is clad in the historical materiality of the city, it emerges as something far more contemporary – as if an old fine cloth had been used to sew a modern dress. The tile is in itself a beautiful piece of ceramic work that scintillates in all the nuances of the spectrum. As a rule I feel I simply have to touch it before I go in.

Lene Tranberg thinks it is more a matter of quality than colour: 'This way of making tiles brings out certain structures in the material and shows how it can vary. It tells us about the phenomenon "clay" in such a lovely way. It removes itself beyond the discussion of whether one likes the yellow or the green that comes out in it, for in a way it is all colours and no colour.'

It gives the otherwise bold gambit of the extension, as Lene Tranberg calls it, an aesthetic sensuousness that functions on slightly different premises from the details in the old main house's chiselled facade. It makes the house 'land' in the city.

The strikingly simple form of the extension is emphasized by the way the roof merges with the facade with no overhang. This is related to the firm's rationalistically conceived projects from the 1990s, such as the Fåborg District Heating Plant, which is composed of clear solid-geometrical figures and expresses a will to let the solution unify into a clear motif without resorting to the frivolity of trying to make the building an image of something that is not there. The easily perceptible form, which is expressed in the sensuousness of a single material, prompts ideas that inside too there is a clear spatiality, that the tall elevation of the roof corresponds to a high-ceilinged interior. In this way the form and finish of the facade become a promise that something equally extraordinary is going on inside.

A workshop atmosphere

The entrance to the museum was formerly through the carriage gate that opens out on to Storgade. It has been moved to the new connecting-passage building, and a diagonal path through the courtyard has been established, from which one can go straight through the porch in the connecting building and out to the square behind, Kulturfirkanten, and Munkevænget, where the museum's parking facilities are. In this way the expansion has created a new passageway in the town.

The programme for the building also included visitors' facilities with a café, lecture hall and workshop, a museum shop and three new spaces for special exhibitions and the collection. The project also involved a renewal of the old building and the furnishing of a room for the museum's collection of icons.

From the porch one goes in either to the museum café and general-purpose room or into the museum shop, where one can buy a ticket. The well-lit ground floor has large windows and has thus been laid out solely to cater for the public and create visual connections within the complex. At the same time it functions as a security barrier for the art, which in the new building is only in the specially fire- and burglar-proof galleries above and in the basement. But the arrangement is not only practical, it also helps to attune one's expectations to what one is about to see.

It has been the intention to create the sensation of a raw atmosphere that takes the art out of the modern art museum's mausoleum-like atmosphere, where the art tends to stiffen into a fixed, final form. Instead the atmosphere of the extension is sketch-like and raw in order to provide a little of the aura of the workshops and studios where the art was originally created. It is subtly done – there are no paint stains on the walls or easels on the floors. Simply leaving out rails and composing materials and transitions so they can be felt lifts the museum space out of the vacuum of the so-called White Cube.

Each exhibition space has its own spatial character and draws daylight in from above in its own way. The gallery of the passage building is narrow, intimate and low-ceilinged, while the large space under the pitched roof fully meets one's expectations of a high-ceilinged hall that matches the exterior of the building. In the basement there is a rather raw concrete space intended for the museum's large collection of the 'Wild' painters of the 1980s but also for changing exhibitions of contemporary art.

The dynamics of the three exhibition spaces of the extension are of course strong, and each pushes the experience of the exhibited art in its own direction. While the small one is ideal for small formats and graphic art and has its own welcoming intimacy, the large gallery is clearly a challenge for the museum unless it exhibits very large works. The basement gallery, on the other hand, with its raw character, has an informal charm that makes it easy to work with for recent art. Nevertheless it is the museum's two stairwell spaces that have become the architectural high points. This is where one's sensory apparatus is aesthetically primed – they open the mind to the world of art.

The stairway that connects the museum shop with the galleries lies in an old extension to the main house and involves a beautiful meeting of materials; raw and coarsely fluted concrete surrounds an elevator tower, while dark, leather-like oiled cross-cut wood lies draped like a soft runner across the steps of the concrete stair, surrounded by whitewashed brick walls. These are meetings of highly characterful materials. As in a Japanese garden you walk on a sophisticated bridge through a landscape of wild forms.

Here there is no dwelling on the individual material quality; it is the composition, the juxtaposition of the coarse and the soft, the moulded and the grown, and what you feel is the time differences in the materials. This matching of the materials until they have fallen into place, until they vibrate, reflects the attuning of the whole effect of the building to the surroundings, which takes place on the grand scale and can be said to be the essence of the phenomenological approach.

A small window hangs like a photograph in the white-plastered outer wall. It has been stripped of all the transitions, the frames and mouldings with which one normally surrounds and mediates the fitting of a window to a wall surface. In this case it appears as a slightly skewed organic hole in the wall. This could only have been done in an existing space; it would have looked false if the window had not been there to begin with. Now it is as if the whole space has been built for the sake of the glimpse the window offers. But in reality the opposite is the case. It is the small, skewed and stripped window that lends the transformation its aura and becomes a co-creator of the atmosphere of the museum.

Sorø Art Museum

Address:
Storgade 9, Sorø

Area:
New construction 1,420 m²
Renovation 810 m²

Client:
Sorø Art Museum

Engineering and client's consultant:
Alectia A/S

Dates:
First Prize in invited competition, 2009
Built in 2010-12

Awards:
Sorø Bevaringsforening 2011
RIBA European Award 2013

Gable. The sober severity of the profile of the building contrasts with a rich materiality. Seen here from the square Kulturfirkanten.

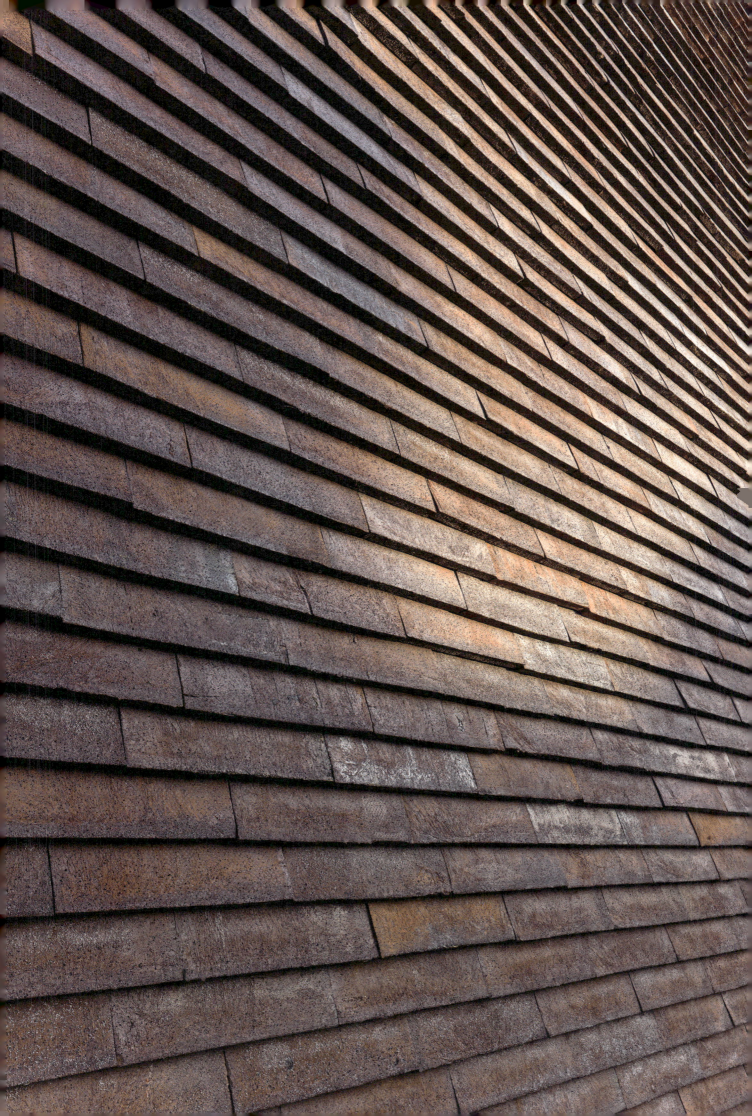

Shimmering. Tiles in many shades are hung on a steel skeleton and not mortared.

Passage. The old main building of the museum with its gate on Storgade leading into the courtyard and the new 'barn'.

Openings. Beneath the roof is the large gallery. Daylight is drawn in from windows in the tilt of the roof, in one half from the east and in the other from the west changing the tone throughout the day.

Run**ner**. Marking the space between the wood and the edge of the step makes the wood appear draped like a textile on the concrete steps.

Subdued. The museum's collection of Russian icons has been installed beneath the roof with exposed rafters in the old main building.

SEB

Anyone who wants to understand what generous architecture can mean to a city should go out to Kalvebod Brygge in Copenhagen. The street is a veritable six-lane motorway surrounded by slow-traffic streets, parking lots and to the east a wall of buildings that cut off the view to the water of the harbour. Not exactly a place you could call congenial, pleasant or beautiful. Not one of the places in the city where you would take pleasure in strolling or skateboarding or where you would go and sit with a sandwich in your lunch break and listen to the wind through the leaves of the trees. It was in fact unimaginable that those kinds of activities would ever take place in the neighbourhood. And perhaps those kinds of nostalgic activities do not belong in a modern city space either, some people might think. Kalvebod Brygge's wide roaring fairway is created for speed, and the only thing you think about there, if you are sitting in a car, riding a bicycle or walking on the pavement, is moving on quickly. It wasn't exactly on the cards that yet another office block – ten storeys and forty-four metres tall – at this desolate place in the city would turn all this on its head.

Leverage

The story of the turnaround of Kalvebod Brygge starts with the Metro, Ørestad and the rehabilitation of Copenhagen from its absolute low point at the beginning of the 1990s. The office blocks along Kalvebod Brygge were the first private investments in Copenhagen's Inner Harbour area after industry and the Navy had abandoned it, and for decades private commerce had avoided the capital. Since 1975 there had been plans for the harbour front with its built-in amenity values to be developed for the equal benefit of commerce, recreation and culture. But the harbour was owned by the state company Copenhagen Harbour (today City & Harbour, owned jointly by the State and the City Council), and the building rights to the first row out to the water were sold with no special requirements for outward-looking functions on the ground floor or urban space quality. The self-confidence of the Copenhagen City Council was at as low an ebb as its finances, so at first when development was to be initiated, architectural sentiments were ignored, since only the fact that anything was happening at all was important for the next stages. Kalvebod Brygge was just leverage. The sale of the site helped to kick-start the building of the Metro and was to link the densely populated inner city with the new Ørestad, where there would be room for lots of income-generating commercial buildings. Kalvebod Brygge was sacrificed in the long-term socio-economic plan, in which the strengthening of the capital was to be a dynamo for the economy of the whole country. In such perspectives, the 'close' values like architectural quality and functional diversity were regarded as trifling concerns.

The architecture became a little more clear-cut and more finely detailed in Schmidt Hammer Lassen's black headquarters for Nykredit and Hotel Marriott's minimalistic wall designed by PLH, but it still consisted of self-sufficient buildings, now just in even larger formats. They ate up the good harbour placing and blocked off other buildings. The tallest spectators set themselves up in the front rank to do battle and made sure they took up as much space as possible because they had the muscle to do so. These are not the types that win many friends.

Although the promenade along the harbour quayside was kept accessible to the public, the area now had so few qualities to offer that the bends that had been built in to give the quay variation rather had the effect of obstacles meant to make people stay away.

A plan for the National Archives

However, the process of attracting venture capital to Ørestad was proving excessively slow, so instead more public institutions were moved out there to kick-start the joint national-municipal project. One of these was the National Archives, which were to lie beside the Danish Broadcasting Corporation headquarters 'DR City', and the German firm Behnisch, Behnisch and Partners won the international competition with a bristlingly spectacular proposal over Lundgaard & Tranberg Arkitekter's rather calmer proposal, to which the expert jury members had in fact pointed. But before the foundation stone was laid for the Behnisch project, it was stopped in 2001 by a new right-of-centre government that wanted to move the Archives to Odense, where the Conservative party chairman Bendt Bendtsen came from.

While the removal was shot down in an internal Conservative feud headed by the law professor Ditlev Tamm, it was realized that the Behnisch proposal would be almost twice as expensive to build, and in the end it was decided to expand the existing Archives at Slotsholmen with a new storage facility on the old Danish Rail freight-yard area at Kalvebod Brygge and thus retain the Archive's association with the capital.

Lundgaard & Tranberg Arkitekter, along with Stig Lennart Andersson's landscaping drawing office SLA, was invited to participate in the State and County Council competition for the area around the future National Archives' storage unit from Bernstorffsgade past Dybbølsbro and Fisketorvet down to Otto Busses Vej. They were permitted to expand their proposal for the commission so it was viewed as an element in a larger infrastructural plan that extended as far as Valby, and they won the competition ahead of three other teams.

Their idea was to create a raised, green, landscape-like pathway where one could walk and cycle undisturbed by the motorized traffic down at Kalvebod Brygge. A hilly landscape that was to provide all the recreative qualities that the first expansion of the area had lacked.

Beneath this 'landscape' one could hide functions that did not need so much daylight, such as the National Archives' storage facilities and a conference centre. The green strip was to be surrounded by varied plantings and wind in and out among a number of tower blocks that would lie like rocks at the edge and absorb the displacements of the terrain. This raised position would be free of the vehicle traffic down at Kalvebod Brygge and would benefit from views of the water. The recreative quality of the harbour was so to speak moved to second place by giving the spectators here a beer crate to stand on. The project recalls the High Line in New York, which was being developed at the same time, but without any of the parties being aware of it at the time.

As an approach to this new urban landscape the plan had two tower blocks.

A glacier between cliffs

The Swedish banking and property group Skandinaviske Enskilda Banken Ejendomme, SEB Ejendomme, acquired the site out towards Bernstorffsgade beside the National Archives and hired the competition winners to design their first domicile in Denmark there. This led to a surprising proposal to divide the property up between two buildings. The organic fusion of landscape and building that the drawing office had worked with earlier, and had so far been most consistently expressed in The Wedge, was now elevated to a new level. The spaces in between the buildings and the landscape were equal components in the new holistic architecture.

In the housing project Charlottehaven from 2001 at Strandboulevarden, SLA and Lundgaard & Tranberg had also had a close collaboration where SLA created a varied garden area with tall wild grasses. But in the horseshoe-shaped project there is a classic hierarchical relationship between urban space, building and courtyard space. The project fills a block that encircles and protects the semi-private spaces of an inner courtyard. In SEB the garden or urban space is a slope that continues the public space of the pavement in between the buildings and conducts the green path up over the roof of the National Archives' storage facility. It rises from street level to a height of seven metres. A serpentine path leads through a 'wild' plantation of, among other things, birch and pine with references to Swedish forests, up to the roof of the Archives' storage unit, where a different landscape space of a calmer and more stylized character takes over.

The ground plans of the SEB buildings are amorphous, and like huge hands or rock walls they cup the landscape. As with a tree in the forest there is no front or back on the buildings, as shown, among other ways, by the fact that their facades are identically finished all the way round. Buildings and landscape become one another's preconditions in a way not previously seen in Copenhagen. With their concave recesses the undulating facades create a lightly protected space between them and suggest a small pocket that gives the urban space calm and prompts one to linger.

The space in between is in many ways the main motif at SEB. It is what makes the composition vibrant. It is so deeply interwoven in the project that it makes no sense to say that one element determines the other or vice versa. True, it is all constructed and artificial, but it imitates and uses the processes of nature in its atmosphere, design and materials.

The landscape comes down between the buildings in a thick flow as if a glacier had for centuries scoured their contours and walls soft and smooth.

But the buildings are not inward-looking and only concerned with the landscape drama they sustain. Around them is a constant flow of cars and bicycles. This is one of the city's heavily trafficked corners, and the soft contours and the sweep of the storey levels around the round corner of the buildings function as a formal response to this motion; they direct the traffic around them. On the diagonally opposite side of the intersection between Bernstorffsgade and Kalvebod Brygge stands the Marriott Hotel building designed by PLH Architects as a squared-off glass wall which in principle could have been infinitely long. It is an example of a building which quite unlike SEB is fully preoccupied with itself, its inner programme and ensuring a view of the water – quite unaffected by anything else going on around it. For it, the city space is what is left over once it has hogged the amenities. It is not itself intended as part of them or to contribute to their quality.

SEB's two buildings, on the other hand, have not only felt their way forward in a delicate and generous correspondence with the surroundings. They are also rational and fulfil their function as office blocks. One of them houses a staff of 650 while the second has been built for renting out with space for 350 workplaces. The bends in the body of the buildings wrench the view free of the neighbouring building, so the employees get the best possible view of the water and the city. And they mask the true extension of the buildings, so it seems to have a far smaller footprint than it actually has. The form came as the result of a wish for a four-metre-wide belt of workplaces along the facade, so that everyone sits close to a window, and the building gets minimal passage space without true corridor areas. Visually there are connections up and down between the floors through a cut along the largest central core. And the sloping landscape is not just a winding ramp up to the roof of the National Archives and the beginning of the quiet green pathway; it also forms the roof of a car park and functions as a collector of rainwater which instead of being conducted to the sewer is recycled for the watering of the bushes and trees of the complex.

A fluid interior

The SEB is in a way about stratification, about rising up above the traffic and creating a topography of different levels with different qualities. The landscape thinking does not stop at the wall of the building. As in The Wedge, the landscape displacements flow in through a glass facade where the white concrete terraces become indoor terraces and stairs in a light terrazzo that runs around the core pillars of the building. The landscape glacier seems to flow in from the outside through the walls of the building and twist around these supports.

The pillars stand close like robust trees inside the middle of the buildings and contain stairs, toilets and printer rooms. As in nature there are no partitioning walls, only staggerings, proximities and openings in a continuous space. The building is thus entirely without corridors and the spaces between the pillars function as distribution passages and informal meeting rooms, while along the outer walls there is a four-metre-deep belt of workplaces. Because the buildings wind around and because the cores stop the gaze, the open spaces never become large unmanageable open-plan offices where the employee can easily feel like an insignificant piece of the totality.

The fluid principle extends not only into the buildings but also into the way they are built. The pillars have been built with a so-called climbing form – that is, the casting has slowly climbed up the tower as it sets. This is a technique developed for places difficult to access such as offshore drilling platforms and is used in large infrastructural and industrial plants. The method has produced a rich, gnarled, raw surface that conveys the forces that rest on these large bearing trunks inside the middle of the buildings. The surface is repaired in a few places because of holes in the casting, but nothing has been done to conceal the traces of the process.

The rawness expressed by the supports is not only symbolically powerful, it is also ruinous for the fine textiles of the bankers' suits. For that reason a steel banister, wound around with leather, has been set up around them. When you touch the building it is soft and warm, while the core speaks of the rising, organic strength that continues up through the storeys in a vertical draught that is visible from the balconies of the storeys above. There one sees how the storey floors are platforms that spread like branches or mushrooms out from the 'trunks' of the pillars. The outermost facade is only a skin that has been drawn around the platforms to maintain the indoor climate. The facade too can be seen to be marked by small recessed bands covered with copper where the storey divisions go, while window bands from floor to ceiling indicate the storey height. In other words by looking at the proportions of the building one can get an idea of its construction and its interior.

Landscape and windings

The industrial and the landscape-like are two orders that work their way through most of the recent projects of the firm. Like the landscape architect Stig L. Andersson in his exhibition *Empowerment of Aesthetics* for the Architectural Biennale in Venice in 2014, one can see it in terms of two principles that have long been separated but should be united: the 'grown' and the 'built'. This unification takes place here at SEB, where geological and biological processes overlap like strata in nature. Perhaps most iconically in the way the leather-wound handrails wind around the raw concrete surfaces of the thick pillars.

By contrast there is nothing organic in the glass of the facade, and unfortunately it becomes something of an empty postulate when a layer of branch graphics appears on the screen windows. This was not necessary. And there is no exterior sun-screening of the building, which is why the windows are covered with a strong green sun filter that gives a rather strange colouring to the light inside.

But these are small blemishes in the SEB building and the 'Bymilen' landscape's innovative composite architecture, which has been of huge importance to the client, the place, the drawing office and Copenhagen. SEB is more than a demonstration of colossal aesthetic energy; it has become a generous private project that turns a city neighbourhood entirely around and creates public values that the public sector would not have been capable of alone.

SEB

Address:
Bernstorffsgade 44-50, Copenhagen K

Area:
27,110 m²

Client:
SEB Ejendomme A/S

Client's consultant:
Emcon A/S

Engineering:
Rambøll Denmark A/S

Landscaping:
SLA and Lundgaard & Tranberg Arkitekter

Artistic consultant:
Finn Reinbothe

Dates:
First Prize in competition for unified plan, 2005
Built in 2008-10

Awards:
RIBA European Award 2011, the Architectural Society's 'Store Arne' Award, 2011, Copenhagen City Council 2011

Silos. The core pillars of the building were cast in so-called climbing form and the storey floors laid around them.

Silence. As soon as you move up the serpentine path between the SEB buildings the noise of the city is perceptibly reduced.

Interwoven. The steps of the landscaping and the staggered interior of the building follow one another in and out through the facade.

Motion. The raw, gnarled concrete with traces of the climbing form of the casting meets the soft windings of the leather handrails.

Challenging. The city space has become popular with skateboarders, who love the fall of the terrain and the sharp edges and ledges of the white concrete.

Framing. With birch and pine, among other features, the varied plantings are unusual for the city but full of references to nature in Sweden.

The Villa in Hellerup

A home is not just a residence. A home is much more than that. A residence is a place to live, a fixed address in a building where you spend the night and perhaps some of your leisure time. But a home is a place where you feel at home, where you are not someone else; it is where you feel you belong and where you hang up your masks when you hang up your coat in the hallway.

The home is the place where your things, habits and history are reflected as patterns in the surroundings. This is where our bodies make their way through living rooms and bedrooms, move furniture around and arrange things until they have found their place, some because we have made a conscious decision on an aesthetic and practical basis, others because that is just where we happen to have put them. It is when we make a home that, like a bird, we furnish our nest with our body. You cannot ask an architect to design a home. It is a task you perform yourself along the way when you live in a place and create a home for yourself, which inevitably follows you like your shadow or reflection.

All the same, it was surprising for me to step into Birgit Lyngbye Pedersen's house in Hellerup for the first time – it was born with so much atmosphere that while the family was moving in it already felt like home.

That feeling does not come from any single factor in the house. As in a Japanese cherry tree in which the beauty is neither in the individual blossom, in the crooked branches nor in the shimmering of a thousand flowers. It is in the relationship between the whole and the part, the colouring of the light and the resulting aura it creates around it. It is a vibrant dialectic between totality and detail.

The house lies in a neighbourhood of very mixed urban quality at Hellerup Harbour. A beach and an intimate harbour atmosphere lie at one end of the road and at the opposite end runs the coastal road Strandvejen, with its urban bustle of shops and traffic. Towards the south lie a number of villas, a sports club with tennis courts, and a low complex of harbour huts; towards the east and west there are more villas, and towards the north a back wall of tall tower blocks.

In the midst of this dense mixture of functions, gardens and buildings on many scales, the villa forms a protected but also extremely flexible setting for the life of its family.

Tree house

The property is small, the house lies close to the road, and at the back towards the east it extends all the way out to a public path. It is surrounded by a lath fence, and rather than saying that the fence is built around the outside of the house, one has to say that the house is built into the fence. All facades are covered with laths from top to bottom like an organic coverlet wrapped around the house uniting it with the garden. From the first and second floor large oblong window bays break out through the lath covering, and towards the west the curtain is drawn all the way back and the house opens up in glass on three floors towards the garden space.

Towards the pavement and the path the light, softly protective lath fence is interrupted on the ground floor level only by the main door in a different material. The door and its frame are weighty and clad in the dark brown copper-zinc alloy tombac, which has also been used to cover the bays on the first and second floor.

At the entrance one has the house's solid in-situ-cast concrete core on one side and a free view of the harbour through a glass wall that encircles the whole ground floor. The counterpoint established here typifies the whole house: the sense of weight and enclosure, of the indoor and the compactness, is consistently balanced by a bright, outdoor openness.

Garden and patio are as in some of the fine single-family houses of the Japanese drawing office Atelier Bow Wow, which are adapted to small – sometimes very small – sites in Tokyo as an integral part of the home, and always have a presence indoors as a mutable, living background. And in the Japanese manner the house can be opened and closed with sliding doors depending on the season.

As suggested by the uniform surfaces of house and fence, the house does not maintain the traditional hierarchy between garden and interior. The spaces of the ground floor can be perceived as going all the way out to the edge of the property. Some of them just happen to be outdoors. The placing of the house on the site was given in advance; formally this is a rebuilding, and the high floor-area ratio could only be preserved by retaining the exterior dimensions of the original villa. This meant, for example, that the garden space on the north side of the house would become a small dark left-over strip unless it was established that the space went from the core of the house out through the glass and all the way to the fence. As Lene Tranberg says of this stratagem:

'We also regard ourselves as landscape architects. It is all architecture; it is just a question of being outside or inside. All that is on the property is a composition based on the core, the column, the tree, the horizontal and the vertical.'

The inspiration for the lath fence and the claddings and the openings of the house comes from the surroundings, from the need for light and a view, and for protection from outside gazes. But the atmosphere that permeates the house from top to bottom comes from the wish to provide a rather special feeling of the unity of garden and home, or as Lene Tranberg expresses it:

'It was clear from the start, before we arrived at the idiom we wanted, that there was to be this feeling when you came inside that something green came in with you, and already here you thought how pleasant it was. The moment you step in, the calm descends.'

With the laths they have taken an element from the surroundings and enlarged it so that the house both blends in with and becomes a baroque, playful version of the neighbourhood's many fences around the villa gardens. It becomes its own universe, a house with its own laws and its own answer to the question of what it means to truly 'live' somewhere. It carries the sense of openness, of being in the garden, also indoors.

In a way it feels like a luxury version of a tree house. The villa takes the form of a number of covered platforms that are more closed or protected at one end, towards the east, and more open at the other end, towards the garden in the west, where a stairway breaks its way up through the platforms and makes them float like islands projecting, some more and some less than others, out into the light. The sensation of greenness, of closeness to the garden, and the feeling of the changing seasons is like that of a holiday home in the countryside. But the closeness to the garden and the outdoor space is simply a bearing quality of the architecture; another and probably more important one is that the house disposes you to togetherness.

Living together

The Villa is designed for a family with older and grown-up children, and the aim was to create a house that embraces everyone and offers tranquillity amidst whatever very different changes the occupants may be going through. It is a place where people are together and where they can drop their guard. On the ground floor and up on the second floor relatively small bedrooms have been installed to which they can also withdraw when they want to be alone. But it is not a house where the teenagers' rooms are small autonomous flats where they can live separate, parallel lives. When you live here, you are all in it together for better or worse, as in a boat or a summer cottage. The bulk of the house thus consists of a large fluid space on three floors with no partition walls.

There is a small kitchen island in connection with the ground floor so one does not need to run up and down when one sits outside in the summer, but otherwise kitchen, dining table, hearth and a two-storey tall bookcase are all together in the communal open space that extends on the first floor all the way out to the exterior walls of the house. Cuts through the storeys ensure internal contact between the different levels, and the cut at the top level is formed as a balcony around the first floor with the result that the space is experienced as having especially high ceilings.

In the window bays, deep wide niches are built in with mattresses where you can sit, lie down or have friends spend the night. They function as a kind of built-in seating milieu, and along with built-in cabinets help to give the house the compact, cosy atmosphere familiar from a boat, caravan or holiday cottage where the furnishings are built in and tailored to the best possible use of the limited space. This leaves a large space where life unfolds as movements among various zones of openness, between outside and inside, between the collective and the private. Not walls but possible activities around the built-in benches, the suspended hearth, the bookcase with TV and the kitchen island define the zones of the space with their own functional focal points. But the openness gives you the feeling that, as in a garden, you can move around in the house with your book or your meal, all depending on the light, the weather and your mood.

All the extra walls, the built-in cabinets, and the 'cathedral ceiling' are clad with a rotary-cut birch veneer. Rotary-cutting, like peeling an apple, means that the wavy markings of the veining and the patterns in the surface of the veneer are never quite identical even though they come from the same tree. The surfaces get an organic look and the wall surfaces have their own distinctive look. The material helps to give a tint and warmth to the house and, like the facade cladding, leaves you with a feeling of being in a wooden hut or that the house is in a hollow tree. The floors here are platforms projecting into the wooden house. They are borne up by a black steel skeleton coated with mottled fluid concrete and their ceilings are coated with a white acoustic plaster.

The marking of the large space with wood veneer helps to establish the sense of belonging together: it unifies the room wherever you may be in it. But one of the veneered ceiling surfaces is further perforated and has been backed with an acoustic fabric to absorb the resonance. The hard floors and large glass surfaces meant that work had to be done to muffle the sound so the acoustics also give you the feeling of being enveloped by the house.

Tortoise

As mentioned, it was necessary if the high floor ratio at the site was to be preserved that the project was regarded as a rebuilding. The exterior dimensions of the Villa come from the earlier house, which had been built as a day nursery and from which two outside walls have been preserved. The drawing office worked to incorporate them visually, but they found it necessary to encapsulate the walls entirely because they had neither enough quality nor character to justify a breach in the new narrative of the house within the fencing.

But the transition between the original house with its almost square ground plan and its later addition of an orangery lives on today in two building-high incisions in the glass facade. They have no direct function but mark the transition between the more covered and more open zones of the house and accentuate the vertical connections of the large spaces in the house. They are a kind of 'negative columns' that give the house a small 'neck'. It lies like a tortoise with its shell to the east and its head in the open air to the west.

It is here too that the levels are bound together by the staircase that cuts through the floors and separates the projecting platforms from the more protected part of the house. The staircase stands free in the space and is seen from the inside as a striking figure silhouetted against the large window surfaces. Diagonally placed steel beams bear its slender steps of steel that seem to float in the air like small repetitions of the platforms.

A lot of care has been devoted to the banister's contouring of the movement up the stairs and around the balcony. No balusters have been put on the corners, so the line drawn by the banister in the air is not fastened to the floor before it has become free of the corner. And as the balusters stand at right angles to the gradient of the stairs, you get a feeling that the guard rail follows the staircase as if it is a ladder that can be raised and lowered.

Along with an exposed steel structure of large I-beams the iron in the staircase area gives an industrial look to the western end of the house. Connotations of railway and shipping mix with these materials and add a different but still magical atmosphere to the warm image of a cave up in a tree.

In some places the laths are used as shutters for the windows. They prevent people looking in, filter the light and evoke memories of the facade. The house folds in on itself.

Balancing act

There are aspects of this house that make it quite central to Lundgaard & Tranberg Arkitekter's activity. The landscape-like conception of the interweaving of indoor and outdoor spaces, and the fluid zones without partition walls are themes one has seen touched on in their far larger educational and office projects. But it is also an exception. The intimate scale of a private home for a daring client has permitted them more of a balancing act with a very high degree of detail. These are far from neutral spaces. The garden space, which is constantly present as a vibrant green background through the large window areas, the absence of walls, the sculptural staircase, the platforms, the built-in bookcase, the rotary-cut veneer, the suspended hearth and the laths are the clear and independent elements that constitute the landscape of the house.

It has all been developed in close cooperation with the client, who is a knowledgeable collector of furniture, and the platforms of the house not only provide potential for many ways of living in the house, they also bring out the sculptural and spatial qualities of the furniture.

It tells us something about the drawing office's courage to challenge its clients and its corollary, this client's urge to experiment, that they ended up covering the whole property and house with nothing more than laths. For there was only one thing the client had written in her list of things she did not want, because it was the most petty-bourgeois and boring: lath fencing.

The Villa in Hellerup

Address:
Onsgårdsvej, Hellerup

Area:
Ground plan 100 m², living area 250 m²

Client:
Birgit Lyngbye Pedersen

Landscaping:
Lundgaard & Tranberg Arkitekter with Julie Kierkegaard

Acoustics:
Gade & Mortensen Acoustics A/S

Dates:
Built in 2014

Calm. Edges and bays are clad with tombac. Larger surfaces are either laths or glass.

Weight. Light-coloured sliding doors in birchwood provide lively surfaces to the villa's core and floors, which are cast in concrete.

Metallurgy. The steel staircase with the floating steps and slender banister are executed in fine metalwork and stand in their rawness with a rich surface of rust and scratches.

Columns of light. Incisions in the facade mark the transition between the more exposed and more covered zones of the house.

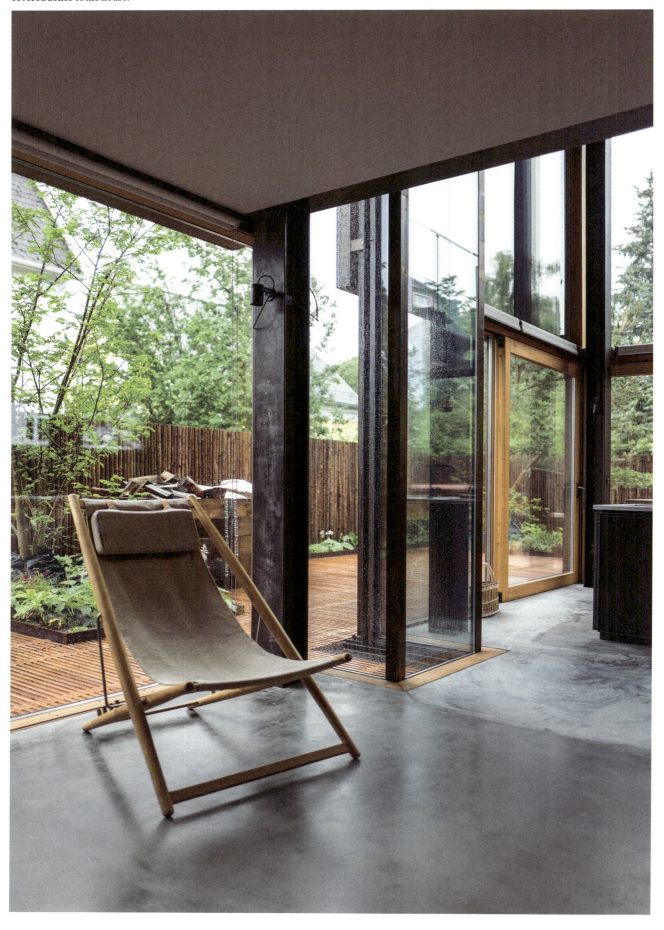

Platforms. Cuts through the floors provide air and contact between the three levels of the Villa. A built-in bookcase extends over three floors and has its own built-in ladder.

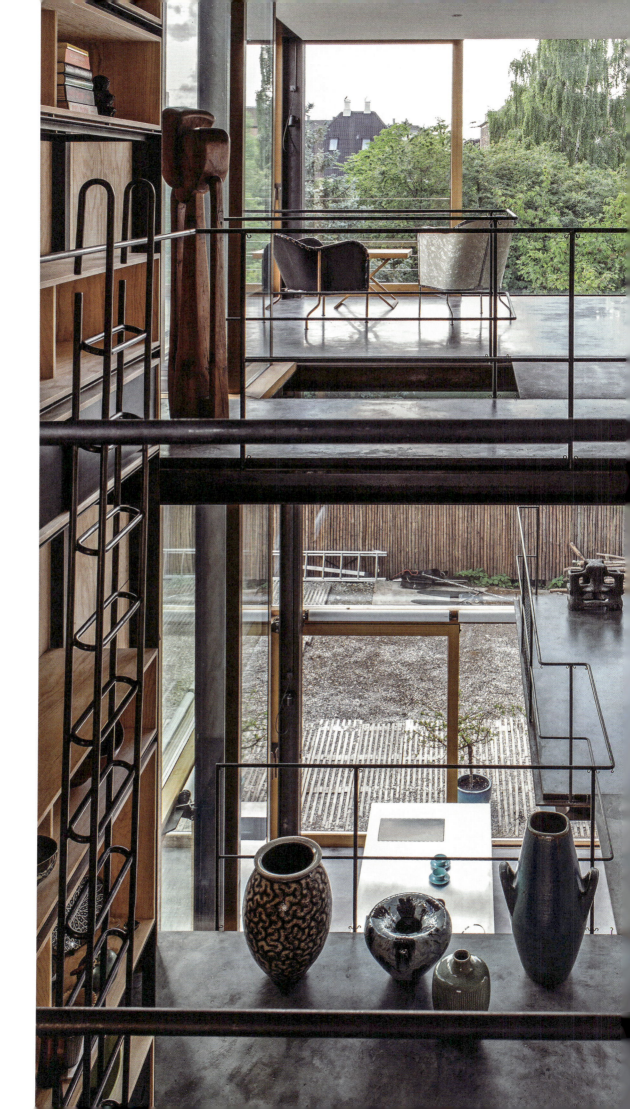

Baylight. There are light-coloured leather cushions in the bays, which function as built-in reading nooks.

Birch veneer. Built-in furniture and seating niches give the house the atmosphere of a boat or caravan.

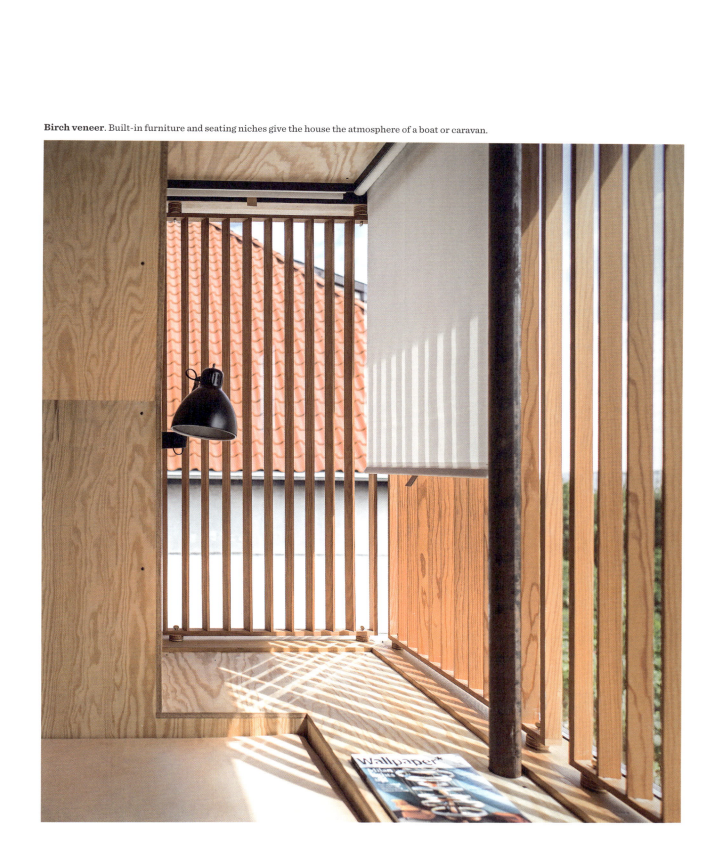

The Warehouse

Facades without relief and with monotonous ribbon windows are perceived as cold or spiritless. Transparent facades can look bare, dead and faceless, while blank facades are seen as unaccommodating, like people wearing sunglasses or with milky-white blind eyes.

Just as we feel and measure buildings with our bodies, we cannot help reflecting our bodies in buildings. We see windows as eyes through which surroundings appear and in which we can read the mood and soul of a building; the front door is a mouth that lets selected parts of the world in, while the back door or basement is, as a rule, where the garbage is sneaked out. But how does one react to The Warehouse at Langelinie, which has windows high and low, small and large, spread out over the facade in an apparently random pattern? It is like a creature with a thousand eyes.

The pattern gives lightness to a heavy facade, and we see the perforation of the facade if not as a game then at least as the result of a process where it is as accidental as in an Emmental cheese whether a hole has become large or small. It gives a personality to the building which at all events is very different from dead or cold glass facades.

The giant brick

The Warehouse lies as the outermost in Langelinie's parade of oblong buildings, all of which take their cue from the height and bulk of Vilhem Dahlerup's warehouse from 1894. Just as Lundgaard & Tranberg Arkitekter is leaving its mark on Copenhagen in the great condensation of our time, or of time itself, Vilhelm Dahlerup was responsible for important buildings in the expansion of the capital at the end of the 1800s – among many others the Danish National Gallery, the Old Stage of the Royal Theatre, the Ny Carlsberg Glyptotek, the Elephant Gate at Carlsberg and the Queen Louise Bridge.

He also designed the Copenhagen Free Port, Langelinie and its first warehouses, but of the last of these only the second and largest remains today. Langelinie and the Central Pier that lies parallel to Langelinie were among the first areas where the rehabilitation of Copenhagen took place from the 1980s on, and they are almost fully developed now. The construction plan for both commerce and housing on the two piers has been modelled on Dahlerup's warehouse.

The property developer ATP Ejendomme secured the last of these warehouse sites and held an international competition for a new office block, which Lundgaard & Tranberg won in 2008. The task was to create a building that conformed to a rigorous German sustainability certification which, among other things, required minimum energy consumption for climate control and the adding of as much value to the building as possible for as little financing as possible.

But while the great depth and meagre daylight conditions of the warehouse motif would have been excellent for keeping goods dry and dark, they are less ideal for office work. You cannot simply transfer a typology developed for one particular function to a quite different one.

The new office building is content to borrow motifs from the old one, such as the attics, which in their day were used for loading cranes; the diagonal cut-off of the building body by the mansard roof; and last but not least the brick as the recurring material expression. This makes the building appear as a solid, heavy mass in a material that anchors it to the earth and the history of the place.

The idea, perhaps a little forced, was that the building should be seen as an oversized brick that an office block had moved into. The perforation pattern in the facade is not inspired by a cheese but by the natural holes that arise during the firing of a brick. So it was also natural for the brick cladding to go all the way up and wrap around the sloping roof surfaces.

The Warehouse can house up to 630 workplaces and is organized so it can naturally house one large company or be split to accommodate three. It is built up lengthwise around an oblong atrium and has two cores with elevators, staircases, toilets and kitchens that divide the building and leave two smaller atria, one at each end. The ground floor has communal facilities installed. At one end there is a canteen, at the other an auditorium.

Harbour architecture

It is a delicate matter, building out to water, and something one might think we in Denmark should have learned by now, having done it for a thousand years. But the conditions for both building and our use of the water have changed greatly. Today our industries rarely have any functional relationship with the water. The new office properties only lie at the harbour to exploit the water and the visual amenities of the open space.

Most, like The Warehouse at Langelinie, have a car park beneath the building, and if you drive a car to work you can walk directly up to the offices without coming into contact with the weather, the city or the harbour. The surroundings have been reduced to a glittering reflection of daylight and a simple window decoration for work functions, which in principle could take place anywhere. For the same reason the new harbour architecture is often perplexed and perplexing. The 'UN City' at the end of the 'Marble Pier' sticks out tellingly in all directions in an attempt to create a meaning with its location.

Lundgaard & Tranberg Arkitekter's office block for ATP Ejendomme has been created subject to the same conditions, the same loss of a functional connection with the place, but at least it tries to make a virtue of the historical aesthetic qualities. It counters the transience of the shipping traffic, the mutability of the water and the architectural lightness of the age with its contrasts. Although the would-be functional has lost its direct link with the location, the expression of the building is like a rock standing against the general inconstancy.

It is clad monolithically in orange-red brick from top to bottom. But the placing of the windows in the facade, typically for the time, has been liberated from the allowances that had to be made earlier for the bearing strength of column-window-column masonry buildings. The masonry is only cladding surrounding a steel-reinforced concrete building that is cheaper and stronger, with more tectonic freedom, than a masonry building. The idea of building up a facade by scattering windows in all sizes over the surface is something one perhaps sees in rather too many places today after the Japanese drawing office SANAA used it in their art school Zollverein in Munich from 2006. But when Lundgaard & Tranberg Arkitekter won the competition for Langelinie in 2008, it was not something that had been seen in this country before.

The windows are in several sizes but everywhere in the same proportions, dimensioned in accordance with different brick courses and all marked with a single raised row of bricks as a frame that only just reinforces the facade relief around the already deep-set windows.

And although the windows on the facade may have a playful or frivolous effect at the viewer's discretion, inside they produce a quite unexpected effect that gives the apparently purely aesthetically motivated randomness a quite different meaning.

Grand Canyon

The main entrance is in the midst of the building, and you are sluiced in beneath a ceiling that seems low in view of the size of the building. But at the middle the space rises in a longitudinal cleft to the full height of the buildings. Floors clad with oak staffs against a dark background slide in and out in a uniformly zebra-striped pattern, which, along with unexceptionable acoustics, all at once holds the space together, shimmers before the eyes and makes the motion up through the storeys rise as in a dizzying flue, which the drawing office, not without reason, compares to the Grand Canyon.

The ground floor continues level with the pier terrain into a large terrazzo cast with potsherds from the pier paving outside. In this sense the floor is a continuation of the city space that we have seen in SEB, the Playhouse and The Wedge, but here the current function of the building requires access to be limited by key cards. There is no extension of the public space in through the building. But the possibility has been allowed for when the current function one day ceases to be relevant.

The walls of the core are black with mortar dyed with lamp black. The original plan was that they were to stand in raw concrete and let the material speak for itself, but they were cast at a time when the contractor, Pihl & Søn, was heading for bankruptcy, which unfortunately meant that the time-honoured firm had begun to slack off on quality. Perhaps a blessing in disguise, for the now dark end walls emphasize only the balconies' sideward progress along the huge 'Grand Canyon' atrium.

The insides of the exterior walls are also – a rarity in Lundgaard & Tranberg Arkitekter's buildings – painted, in fact painted white. It was thought necessary to create a sense of calm, as so much is going on in the stave cladding of the ceilings, in the wooden floors, the balconies and the windows, with their many levels. But along with the white ceiling at the very top, this helps, as in the Villa in Hellerup, to show how the exterior wall is a shell pulled across the cores and the floors.

Pictures at an exhibition

If the tall interior cleft was the first great surprise, the effect of the many windows is the second. Water has a fantastic influence on us. It is always changing, and it reflects the light according to wind, cloud cover and waves, so it never remains quite the same. But in conjunction with the distinctive perforation, the water makes the building into a wonderful lighting system. The windows create a richly varied incoming play of light and shade of the kind one can see through the treetops in a forest.

The result is a more varied lighting than I have experienced behind the facades of any of the harbour's other recent commercial buildings with their use of monotonous ribbon windows from floor to ceiling. The smaller window area also means in quite practical terms that a more natural and varied daylight enters the Warehouse, since it permits the use of a more transparent window glass with less sun filter and without too much heat from the sun. And for the exploitation of the area it means that desks can be placed closer to the facade without the staff feeling that they are 'falling out'. No less importantly, the windows crop the view into small framed pictures.

It is part of the basic training of any photographer that a foreground gives depth and space to a picture and that the cropping means everything for the subject. That the same goes for a view of otherwise open surroundings is something one can learn from the Warehouse at Langelinie. The facade frames and crops the panoramic view of the pier, so it becomes possible to relate to what is seen. The detail gives a scale to the otherwise scaleless view. The many sizes of such details high and low also permit the views to be experienced as pictures at an exhibition; here it frames a treetop, there a crane, a chimney or part of a fort. Each thing in the surroundings is given more attention and more significance by being cropped out than when the view is seen panoramically.

And of course the view is formidable if you simply cycle out to the point of Langelinie to eat an ice cream at the kiosk. But it is also difficult to absorb. The compositions created by the framing create a dramatization that makes each detail more striking, more charged with meaning.

Contrasts

The atmosphere of the building from outermost to innermost is all about contrasts: the dynamic contrast between the fleeting mutability of the water and the firmly anchored rock face of the facade, between the mass and its sparkling lightness in the perforation of the windows, between the relatively low floors and the deep vertical draught, between the bustling diversity of the projecting storey deck and the unity of the overall span of the cleft, between the great open view and the narrow cropping of the windows, between being part of a small local working unit and a large collectivity.

It has a consistent weight all the way from the expression of the facade to the cores and the dark steel columns and yet at the same time an incredible lightness because the decks simply hover and have this light, bright wood cladding. It is something very strong and highly articulated wrapped around something very delicate.

The Warehouse unifies this world of dramatic contrasts. These are neither artificial nor postulated contrasts. Care has been taken with the transitions, and the spatial effects are mutually determining. The low-ceilinged storeys have a cave-like intimacy along the firmly protective outer walls, while the cleft lets the space breathe and gives it a grandeur that responds to the surrounding view.

Several of 3XN's harbour buildings, the UN City, the DFDS terminal and the Lighthouse in Aarhus, have an idiom and materials evocative of modern shipping, but funnily enough Lundgaard & Tranberg Arkitekter's solid warehouse interior produces a stronger feeling of being on the open sea, at the mercy of the elements and protected by a strong hull.

Despite a richly varied spaciousness, the building has an ability everywhere to manifest as a totality. You can always see something of the outer shell and the view, and when you look out of the windows you always have a frame of the orange-red brick cladding of the facade. As in a forest, the elements are everywhere the same, and yet the combinations make it changeable everywhere.

It is a building full of surprises. You cannot guess from the facade how it is organized, how the space is disposed behind its bouncing windows or how it is experienced from within. But once you have been inside and experienced the effect of the many window frames, seen the play of the light on the floors and felt the great space of the cleft and afterwards seen the building from the outside, the effect is clarification that it could not have been otherwise.

The Warehouse, Langelinie

Address:
Langelinie Allé 47, Copenhagen Ø

Area:
Total 28,300 m², 16,500 m² of which above ground

Client:
ATP Ejendomme

Engineering:
COWI A/S

Artistic consultant:
Finn Reinbohte

Dates:
First Prize in international project competition 2008
Built in 2012-15

Viewer. Modern office blocks do not have much to do with a harbour placing, as reflected by their facades. They simply see it as a view.

Systematic. The proportions of the window openings follow the stacking of whole bricks, vertically and horizontally.

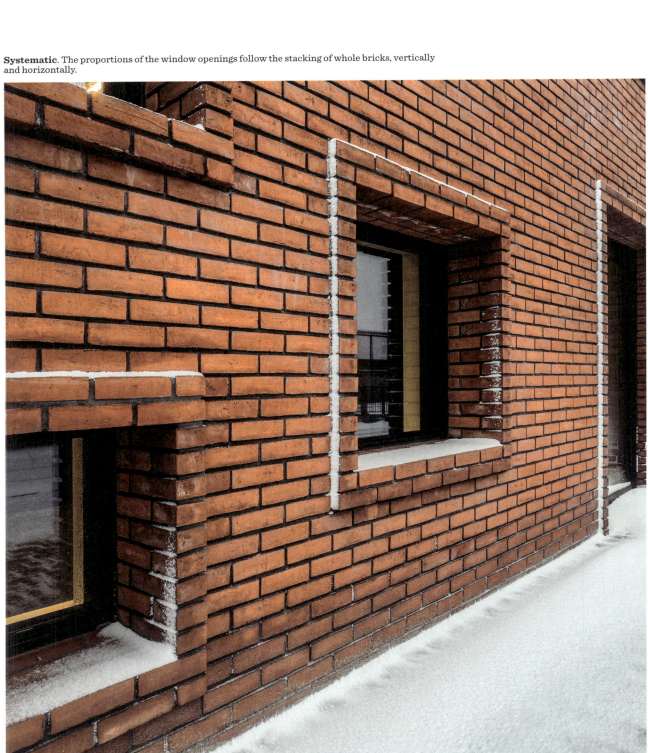

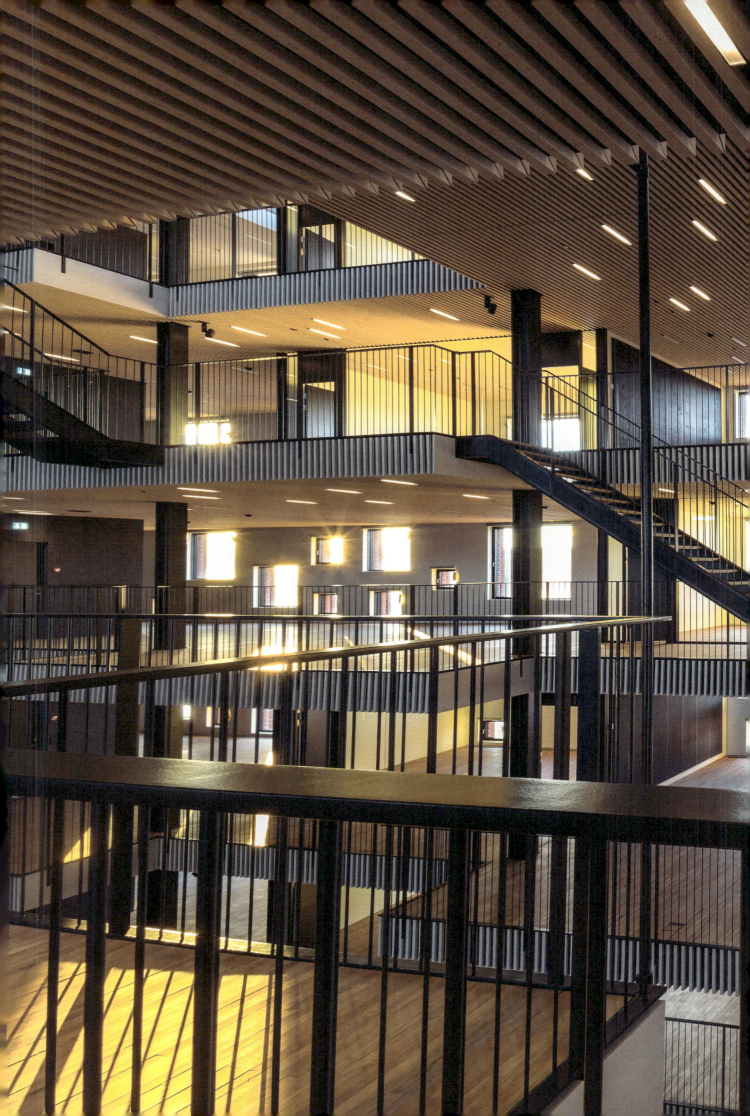

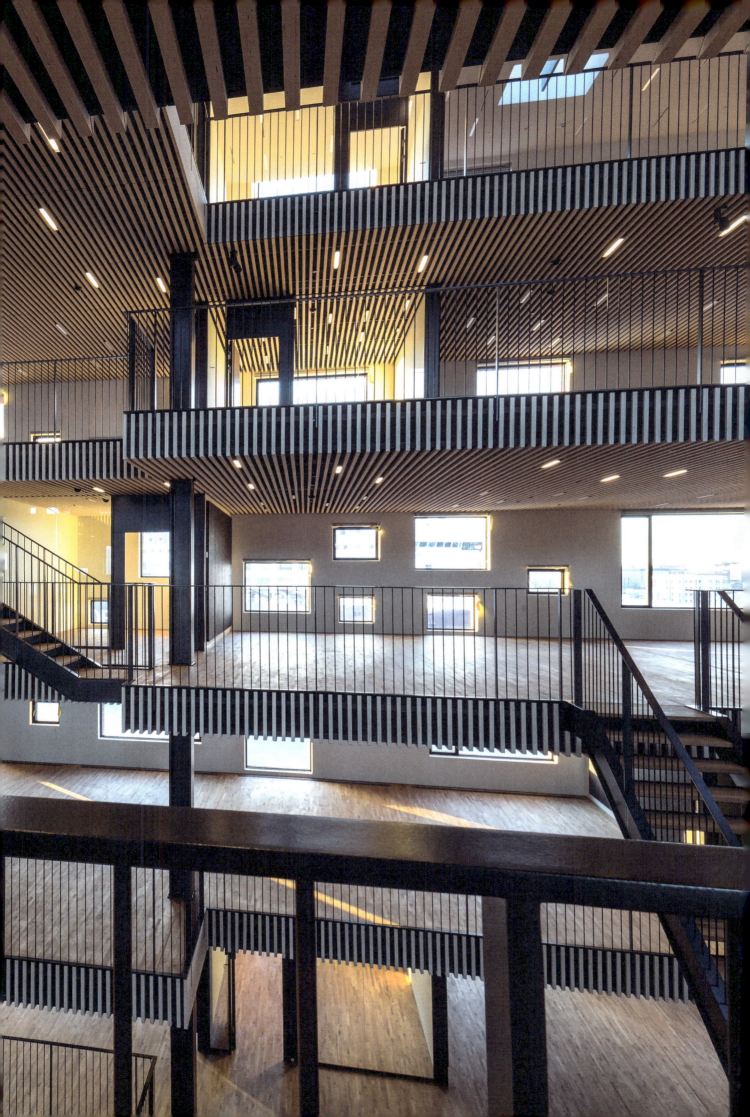

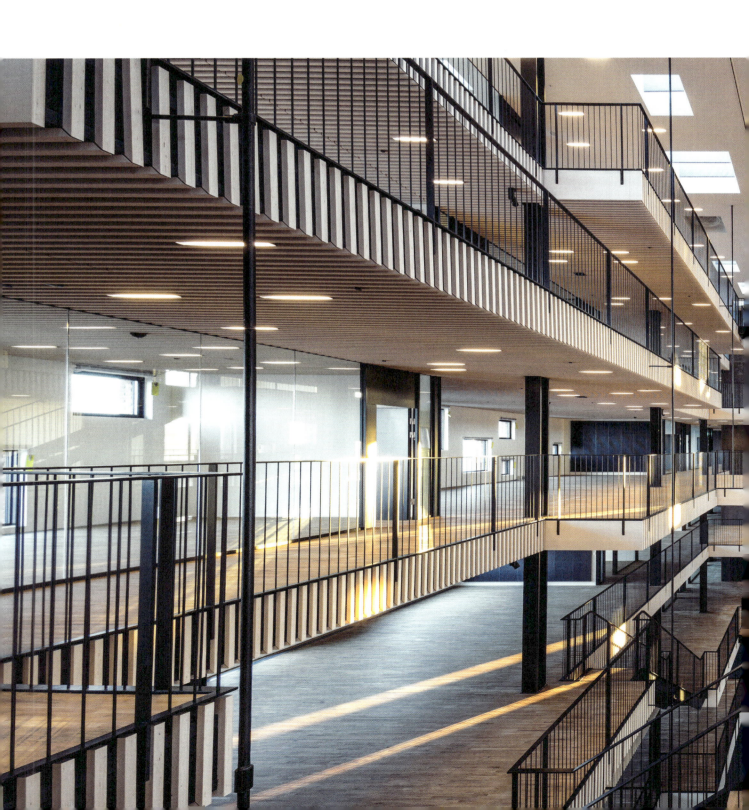

The cleft. The Warehouse is designed with natural ventilation. This has made the unusually narrow storey partitions possible because there is no need to fit ventilation pipes in the ceilings.

The shell. The white colour of the outer walls and the crowd of window openings continue around the ceiling.

Axel Towers

Copenhagen's characteristic skyline is a birthday cake. The base is formed by the ordinary houses of the city of four to five storeys, topped with an icing of high tiled roofs that can reach a height of twenty-five metres, and above these the birthday candles of power, copper-clad spires and towers. The history of the cake goes back to the time of the entrepreneurial building client and Renaissance king, Christian IV, and has been expanded with new towers and airy spires all the way down to the latest version of Christiansborg Palace from 1927. The birthday cake image is a heritage that only began to be retouched after World War II. Just outside the old city nucleus came true high-rises, like Arne Jacobsen's elegant seventy-metre-tall SAS Hotel from 1960, while several later additions in the 1970s were clumsier square candles without the necessary sophistication required earlier to share in the creation of the festive Copenhagen birthday cake.

In the 2010s the city has seen a growth in population of some 10,000 people a year, all of whom must find places to live, work and get an education. In the harbour, closed-down industrial and commercial areas are exploited, and on the island of Amager natural areas are commandeered, but to ensure that the population growth will not result in a corresponding pressure on the road network, some of the adaptations also take the form of a concentration of the already-developed areas around the nodal points for public transport. At selected points offices, hotels and housing are therefore allowed to shoot up in the form of high-rises. And so once more intensive construction activity is evident on the horizon above Copenhagen – the new 'candles' of power, which depending on their quality either erase or renew the old image of the birthday cake.

This is where the project Axel Towers intervenes as the most fairytale-like contribution from our time so far: a whole cluster of five partly grown-together round towers of various heights up to sixteen floors and sixty-one metres. Just opposite the main entrance of the Tivoli Gardens it forms a little triad along with Axelborg with its small spire and Jacobsen's SAS Hotel.

The cluster

The cluster of towers is clad in copper alloy tombac, and the facade has been given a low relief of fins which both function as a sunscreen and give the tower surfaces a rich texture – something totally absent on the other side of the street in the soulless glass facades in the drawing office Transform's rebuilding of the House of Industry and in Pei, Cobb and Freed's project Tivoli Corner, which seems oddly distant and non-material.

But the tone of the city is expressed in the copper-coloured facades of Axel Towers, which wrap a layer of the familiar around a richness of form and a building ensemble the like of which has never been seen before in the city.

The composition of the towers is oriented slightly towards the east and Tivoli, such that the complex lies as an escalation from Vesterport Passage (as the last stretch of Vesterbrogade up to the City Hall Square is called) and concludes in a steep encounter towards the west and Jernbanegade, which in fact has the formally closest relative of the towers in the Circus Building. But if the composition is slightly oriented in one direction, the round towers themselves are directionless and with a narrow passage just break free of the block that the earlier buildings terminated. They stand like dense, independent clusters of trees in a grove at Axeltorv and as such have neither front nor back.

Instead they help to nuance and enrich the public space. They have moved a little further out into the city space than the earlier building but give even more back to the city with their in-between spaces. Behind the towers there is a raised inner city garden with trees in large basins.

Above the garden a wonderful vision of circles rises. The convex towers have grown together with bridge structures by way of concave connecting buildings which thus form what one might call negative towers. As in the SEB project the space between the buildings is a fully valid part of the architectural stratagem. It is in this undulating interspace that the project seriously becomes generous, that it addresses itself to and gives something away free of charge to others than its primary users.

Both on the terrain and in the city garden there are outward-looking functions with restaurants and shops, but it is the three broad sets of seating steps that provide access to the garden, which is perhaps after all the project's most socially important contribution to the urban space. This is where one can sit, elevated slightly above the crowd, hang out and watch people.

The ramparts

At the same time that the project that creates a hitherto unseen typology, it draws on an old narrative and attempts to reintroduce some of the older qualities of the place. The landscape-like raised city garden plays on the former ramparts that ran as a ring around the city with bastions and a moat and whose topography and blue-green spaces can still be seen all the way from the historically restored Citadel in the north to the undomesticated Østre Anlæg park, the neatly arranged Botanical Gardens and the romantically winding Ørsteds Park over the hilly terrain of the Tivoli Gardens to the Christianshavn Rampart, which continues its rounds in the idealized urban landscape of the 'Free City' of Christiania.

It was Vilhelm Dahlerup who ensured in his time that the ramparts were preserved as a green, recreative belt around the inner city when the decision was made to abandon the city wall and expand the city with the '-bro' neighbourhoods (Nørrebro, Vestebro, Østerbro). The results were not equally good everywhere, and the sequence, among other things, was interrupted by the square Israels Plads and the buildings there, and by the railway, which at first had its terminus where the Palads Theatre lies today at Axel Torv.

The raised urban space between the towers is thus a direct reference to the rampart terrain, while the round towers are seen by the drawing office as a kind of meditation over the watchtowers that could have stood on the ramparts. As in The Warehouse and the Sorø Art Museum, the architectural approach borrows its weight and authority from the history of the city. But not in the sense that any attempt is made to restore a former glory. The history only becomes a pretext for liberation from the arbitrary and lightweight nature of the potential approaches of today in order to establish something which, besides its social functionality, can root us with the weight of meaning to the place. How much more lightweight, simplistic and transitory architecture can become without such a temporally embracing gesture can be seen precisely in the House of Industry and Tivoli Corner.

Axel Torv is a place that exudes modern history. For example, it was here that Ole Jastrau in Tom Kristensen's novel *Hærværk* ('Havoc') went to the 'dance restaurant' in the middle of the night and where department stores and other night clubs later appeared. In the first half of the twentieth century this new neighbourhood between the City Hall Square and the Central Station was one of the city's fanciest places – the most fashionable with the highest property prices. The 'cake base' of the city has been extended here with block developments out over Copenhagen's old ramparts, not with narrow lanes as in the medieval city but rather with broad boulevards and greater scope for making room for the scale and speed requirements of new means of transport in the creation of an effective modern city.

A century later it was no longer the dream of ten-lane boulevards that drove the development of the city but the wish for rich recreative urban spaces for more or less unprogrammed sojourns. The number of lanes in Vesterports Passage has been reduced, and instead the pavement has been widened so it can make room for a wealth of places to spend time and for outdoor serving from the cafés of the area.

The design of the recreative urban space here and in Axel Towers is an element in the international competition among cities to have the highest quality of life, in which Copenhagen has become one of the front-runners and, in the rankings of a range of magazines, as a rule ends up at the top.

Corner offices

It is profoundly impressive that the firm survived presenting a client with the idea of five towers instead of a closed box and persuading him to build them. All other things being equal, facades are expensive, and although round forms produce the smallest surface in proportion to the enclosed area, the ratio of facade square metres to inner area is rather high in Axel Towers.

The project has been financed by three pension funds, and most of it serves as offices for the legal firm Gorrissen Federspiel. The two lowest floors house shops and restaurants, and on the tenth floor there is a sky bar and restaurant.

The rationale behind the round office towers is, as with SEB, to get as much daylight as possible to all the workplaces. A bonus is that everyone gets a corner office. Being able to sit in a corner with the best view is a value that can tempt the best staff to your company. And Axel Towers has primarily been built for the lawyers of Gorrissen Federspiel, who battle with other similar firms to attract the best manpower. The design will not only give the lawyers workplaces in the sky above the city; it will also give them new ways of organizing. It is an experiment.

The five mutually evolved towers are a modern counterpart to the dragon spire of Christian IV's Stock Exchange building from 1625 with its four interlaced dragons' tails. This symmetrical building celebrated mercantilism, which is meant to strengthen the prosperity of the realm through trade with other countries, and Axel Towers celebrates the immense complexity of the late modern rule of law which makes the interpretation of legal texts crucial to the financial failure or success of firms.

But more than simply baroque images that over the centuries become national heritage, the age of democracy demands that its buildings are in principle transparent, permeable and demotic all at once. In this case they have not been built by a monarch to strengthen the trade of his citizens and the prosperity of the nation but rather as foundations to secure the pension savings of ordinary wage-earners.

Christian IV was a builder-king who used the beauty of architecture as a resource in the drama of power. He knew the power of beauty. Today we live in an aesthetically poorer age, in which architectural savvy is not necessarily widespread among those who have the power to build. Everyone can see when a building fits in and feels right, but those who have to pay for it perhaps do not always have the ability to imagine it.

In Axel Towers, for example, it was an uphill struggle for the architects to keep the fins of the towers. The low reliefs of the facade are a crucial element in creating the feeling that the building is directed towards the surrounding world. But it is of course more difficult and more expensive to make than a plain facade. The client was only grudgingly persuaded because the fins are an element in the sun-screening, so it would take a quite different air-conditioning system and new engineering calculations of the energy consumption of the building to change them. Practical arguments always trump aesthetic ones in building projects, so a fusion of the two is necessary in the design phase.

But it is far from given that a project will end with the consistency that the architect wants. The client for Axel Towers, for example, wanted the facade to change at the top around the roof terrace so there could be smoked glass and room for the firm's logo.

Here too the drawing office had to struggle to preserve the architectural quality of the project. This was a general contract where the architect refers to the building contractor, who is responsible to the client. This construct in reality denied the drawing office control of the project and meant that the drawing office did not have as much supervision as it was used to, and this has resulted in some solutions they would have stopped to change if they had been present. The most conspicuous of these is that the terminations of the towers, their top edges, are not round but polygonal. This may seem like a minor detail, but it is precisely the small details that play together and make a project land safely or almost miss the runway. The main device is the cluster of round buildings which with the in-between buildings inscribe a composition of negative and positive spaces in alternating concave and convex forms. When the parapets at the top of the towers suddenly become angular, a different formal language emerges and they tell a different story – among other things, a story about a contractor and a client who went a long way to follow a fantastic idea that they nevertheless proved not to have fully understood.

As Lene Tranberg says: 'In this project we came a long way with a strong architectural vision. But now and then there is a lack of architectural culture among the clients, an inadequate understanding of the responsibility one has for the city and the coming generations.'

Architecture may well be a game, but it must not become a silly one. It is also serious. It has to be able to accommodate a wealth of situations, so it is not just a matter of creating some amusing shapes but of making something that is so strong in its own right that it can stand long afterwards for the benefit of other people than those who had it built, and for quite different purposes.

Axel Towers

Address:
Axeltorv 2, Copenhagen V

Area:
40,200 m2, 23,000 m² above ground and 17,200 m² in a parking basement in five floors. Shop area 4,700 m²

Primary user:
Gorrissen Federspiel (14,000 m²)

Client:
Norden Ejendomme / ATP Ejendomme, Industriens Pension and PFA Pension

Client's consultant:
Rossenconsult A/S

Engineering:
Procon A/S and Züblin A/S

Artistic consultant:
Finn Reinbothe

General contractor:
Züblin

Dates:
Built in 2013-16

Welcome. Axel Towers lies on the old ramparts and forms an inviting transition between the medieval city and the more modern part of the town. Along with Arne Jacobsen's SAS Hotel it forms a portal on arrival at the Central Station.

Process. Axel Towers' tombac facades shone like gold during construction. Six months later they had turned dark brown.

A concluding essay

The open programme

To insist on a style is to lock oneself into an interpretation of the world. It does not need to be the right one in any other sense than that you have done it before and intend to do it again. And so some of the world's most famous architects, from Norman Foster through Zaha Hadid to Frank Gehry, can be recognized for a style on which they insist as a brand, irrespective of whether what they design is a museum of art, a commercial building or a stadium. They insist that their individual formal world has an ideological content, that with the obstinate language of their projects they are influencing the users – whether this is truly the case or they are just filling the world with even more self-reference. Lene Tranberg also speaks of insistence, but she is thinking of something else. She is not talking about filling the world with a particular aesthetic. She is talking about insisting to the client: 'If you are not invited, then you must invite yourself. That is the code word. You must insist that you have something to offer.'

This means for example attention to the effect of the building as part and as totality. The first known architectural theorist, Vitruvius, in his books from 25 BCE, called the adaptation of the architecture to the function and status of a building *decor* – 'that which is fitting'. This was a view of the totality that did not go beyond the bounds of architecture. But in the Renaissance, when his writings exerted their true influence, among other ways through the treatise of Leon Battista Alberti, which is based on Vitruvius, *decor* is reinterpreted and devalued. First there is geometry, and then there is 'decoration', as Alberti calls it, considering it something external and arbitrary. The view of architecture as something that only relates to purely spatial relations was further strengthened with Functionalism, which with Adolf Loos's famous text 'Ornament and Crime' from 1908 relegated the already dethroned 'decoration' to an inferior stage of civilization.

But when we experience in something a harmony of large and small, when a building feels consistent all the way from the surroundings through its exterior lines to its internal details, so that it all falls into place, it takes on a special meaning. Someone has made an effort to ensure that you can have this particular experience. This is in many ways exactly what Vitruvius meant by *decor*. In order to understand the concept, he thought, the architect had to know something about everything, not just about construction techniques, craftsmanship and economics but also about art.

As an architect you must insist, says Lene Tranberg. You work for other people's money, but you must take on the responsibility for knowing better. It is like going to the dentist. Although it is the patient who is paying, there is no point if the dentist leaves it to the patient to decide where and how the drilling is to be done. In the face of powerful clients and ditto builders a good architect must insist on knowing better. That takes knowledge. Technical knowledge. A good architect must therefore know in detail how to put a building together. Otherwise the cohesion is not achieved.

'A building must be generous.

It should give more than it takes.

It should take part in the life of the city and give something away for free.'

So goes the motto for Lundgaard & Tranberg Arkitekter. It expresses a mode of thinking that has followed the drawing office since the beginning.

The idea that a building can be generous subscribes to the tenet that architecture is not just arbitrary form but affects our lives aesthetically and socially. It is a credo that not only applies to the architects and their work but aims at an unknown user and defines the framework for what to expect from a collaboration with this drawing office.

It may well be that the client's wishes, the architect's competencies, the builder's abilities and the constraints of economy and legislation to a great extent determine how much is built, how and for what, but not exactly what is built or who it will concern. The credo is aimed outward at an as yet undefined collectivity. When Lundgaard & Tranberg speak of generosity, it is the building that must be generous. It must give something away for free.

In an opening debate in connection with the exhibition *The Art of Many* in the Danish pavilion at the Venice Biennale in 2016, Bjarke Ingels warned against narrow-mindedness in Danish architecture, or being too concerned with bringing out the right growth rings in one's wood cladding, as he put it. The materials and the moods they evoke may be important, he emphasized, but architecture has so many more important tasks, so much greater potential to change and improve people's lives, that the architect must apply his primary energy at a different point.

This was not aimed specifically at Lundgaard & Tranberg Arkitekter but at a material fetishism that he believes has sometimes blinkered Danish architecture. Site-specific architecture, he opined, imposes a lot of restraints on itself that perhaps preclude the solution that may be of most benefit to everyone.

In other words the criticism of the phenomenological approach to architecture is that it is conservative and preoccupied too much with how the world looks and too little with how it might be. Architecture is for Bjarke Ingels a practical utopia, a dream of how the world could be that is realized every time one builds; science fiction becoming science fact.

Bjarke Ingels is right in his critique of site-specific architecture if it only mediates materials and volumes between neighbouring buildings. But it is also a 'straw man' argument, for what he is criticizing is a very poor manifestation of the sense of place. It is as if instead of trying to strengthen the dynamics it is possible to create at the place, you cancel them out. By simply communicating what is there you risk stifling the spirit of the place. You have to add something new. When Heidegger emphasizes how a temple on a mountain can evoke the 'mountain-ness', it is certainly not done by building a smaller mountain on top of the mountain. The temple is radically different from the mountain, and it is the relation between the two that is art.

As shown by Lundgaard & Tranberg's best works, it is always the interplay of contrasts and contexts that evokes the potential of the place.

Bjarke Ingels's drawing office BIG has itself created a phenomenally place-adapted project in the Museum of Shipping in Helsingør. The commission here was to create a museum in the old dry dock of the shipyard, and that the building was not to tower over the terrain, in order to protect the world heritage site Kronborg Castle. Instead of filling in the dock and covering it over, BIG's idea was to preserve the open dock and instead build the museum around it and use it as the museum's inner courtyard. In this way the dock became the museum's biggest exhibit. At the same time they created a round tour of the museum that starts all the way up in the terrain with a ramp that zig-zags in two-storey bridges down through the dock and continues in to the exhibition spaces around it.

The bridges apparently have a thin profile, because it has been possible to conceal the bearing steel structure in its tall slanted railing. The contrast between the weight of the concrete dock and the sloping span of the visually light bridges, between the flat glass walls and the gnarled concrete, between the intervention and the history of the place are all excellent elements in the intervention's understanding of the spirit of the place. That it has required giant steel anchors and hundreds of millions of kroner to ensure that the groundwater does not blow the emptied dock off like a cork is another story.

They have succeeded in surrounding the dock with an almost invisible glass wall, so the main story is about the raw concrete bulk of the dock contrasting with the minimal rigour of the bridges.

But the evocation of the close scale partly misses the mark, for example in the aluminium coatings of the diagonal railing of the bridges which covers the bearing steel structure. They function as sun reflectors that grill the visitors on their way into the museum. They are a constructional device that does not have a coexisting bodily correlation.

It is otherwise such an excellent approach that has been found here, and yet one fails to see how the feeling created is followed up in the detail so that the building can also be experienced on an entirely intimate scale. The bodily dimension of architecture is not about looking luxurious. It is about the feeling that the architecture exists for the people who are present in it.

Far out in the forest

If the phenomenologist Martin Heidegger saw the artwork as an opening in the world, it was because he thought of it as a clearing in a forest. 'The Origin of the Work of Art' is a lecture that comes from the collection *Holzwege.* The title plays on the phrase 'auf dem Holzweg sein', which means you have gone astray, where the 'woodland path' is applied to a dead end in the forest where the forest workers have been led into a clearing and not along a path that leads out of the forest. Heidegger wrote and hiked in southern Germany and the large tracts and hilly terrain of the Black Forest. When you come to a clearing there you can pause on your hike, because the forest becomes visible to you; the gradient of the terrain means that you can look out over it and perhaps for the first time see where you have been walking and where you are going. While you are still in the forest you get a temporary overview and a feeling for your position in it. Heidegger thought that existence as a rule was full of everyday chores, full of things you have to relate to, such as the limited-vision hike among the trees in the dense forest, but that the work of art could be just such a clearing in whose existence you had the possibility of experiencing it in a wider context.

Lundgaard & Tranberg Arkitekter's buildings are not clearings in the sense that they leave sites from which a new world view can rise – that was exactly the Heideggerian understanding of art that the composer Karlheinz Stockhausen expressed to the outrage of the surrounding world when he called the terrorist attack on the World Trade Center in New York on 11 September 2001 the world's biggest artwork. Formally, perhaps he was right. But in most people's ears art has something to do with fictional entertainment and in all instances is something that fundamentally has a positive value and is thus not something that can be associated with grief and anger at the mass killing of thousands of innocent people.

Architectural art is of course edifying. But Lundgaard & Tranberg Arkitekter's sometimes surprising, innovative architectural works have such an internal connection with their surroundings and their functions that they can in fact have the effect of openings in the forest from which, if nothing else, you can unfurl anew the city, the architecture and the times.

All the buildings reviewed here can be said to transform the understanding of their places or functions: the landscape-like interweaving of The Wedge with the campus landscape and its pauses and passages; the Tietgen Hall of Residence's celebration of the community, which at the same time provides an insistent plenitude in an urban non-place; the opening up of the harbour front at the Playhouse and Kvæsthusbroen to widely different social frameworks for ways of being in the city; Sorø Art Museum's interweaving with the structure and materiality of the town and its attempt to elevate the viewing of art out of the modern art museum's White Cube and into a more living atmosphere; SEB's interweaving of city space, landscape and office block; the Hellerup Villa's consistent interweaving with the garden space and its focus on the home as a place for being together; the spatial contrasts of The Warehouse and the framing of its view; and Axel Towers' reuse of the fortification ramparts as motif, which weaves the wish for office workplaces together with an urban centre and a venue for unprogrammed meetings.

These are not just generous buildings in the sense that most of them open up for others than the primary users; they not only deliver answers to the fundamental questions, such as what it means to live as a family, to be a young student, to work in an office. They also attempt to open up these unambiguous relations in an architecture that points beyond function. They all express a will to find new ways of interweaving past and present and reversing the hierarchy in architecture between functional spatiality and artistic atmosphere.

This makes them works of art in the Heideggerian sense. They are openings in existence that permit us to look at it in a new way. By no means as radically and urgently as the terror attack of 11 September, which opened up an abyss to a new, sombre world order of unceasing revenge for revenge. But they are architecture that has arisen in this age of terror, and although we are speaking of two widely different spheres and scales, there is still in the architecture reviewed a core of human edification that lights the way in a dark age when one is otherwise tempted to meet violence with violence. Care for the place, how buildings meet their surroundings, how people move and live are not in principle the concern of the client, but here they contribute to an architectural humanism. Architectural value is many things. But it is nothing if it is not first and foremost humanist.

As Lene Tranberg says: 'When you install a building in the surroundings in which you happen to be, then the nature of the exercise is not to point the finger at the others but to try to interweave with them. Someone has once made an effort, while others may not have had the chance to do so. But we must live in these mixed contexts where everything is given in advance.'

The point is that Lundgaard & Tranberg Arkitekter are not creators of new worlds. When one thinks of the city and the landscape as places where everything is given and the aim is to discover and bring out their potential, the idea is not to change the world but to find and emphasize something that was not visible before.

The interesting thing is that this attitude perhaps nevertheless changes the world more than the confrontational one that wants to break it down and create something radically new.

The Dutch architect Rem Koolhaas said in 2006 in connection with the unveiling of the building society Realdania's large harbour project, later named Blox, which his drawing office OMA created in Copenhagen, that their aim with the designs was to give the Danes some opposition. They conjured up a building that challenged the whole focus on adaptation and fine details and instead had a feeling for the major functional connections and historical interfaces in the city. It would be a shock, he said. He meant that we are sleeping in a welfare bubble with our design, which glosses over all differences and keeps our cities in artificial museum-like costumes. He is interested in a 'dirty realism' that reflects the economic and political forces that impact on construction and society.

But amidst this critical truth-seeking there is also a weak-willed cynicism that quite unnecessarily ends up distorting the given. Blox is a spatially highly sophisticated and interesting project, and its fundamental stacking and large lattice girders have a superficial constructional resemblance to the Playhouse. But it is consciously completely devoid of the latter's feeling for interweaving with its surroundings, not least Christian IV's Brewhouse. After processing by the authorities and demands from the citizenry, however, Blox was pushed forward to a greater distance from the Brewhouse, reduced and partly attuned in colour to the surroundings. But materially the building still appears as a radical contrast with its historical environs. If all buildings express a hope or a dream, a vision of the world, then Blox expresses a dream of another place in a time other than the one it has landed in.

Here the architect demonstrates, like a critical know-all, that harmonizing one's expression with the surroundings is in reality an attempt to gloss over and blur the economic, technical and power-related differences between then and now. Blox is generous with its many playgrounds, urban spaces and transit routes, which interlace a wealth of urban functions with its building mass. It cross-programmes, as it is called, when it lets several functions overlap in the same building strategy and thus becomes like a small city within the city. But it is ungenerous in its historical arrogance, by only insisting on itself and its time. It is self-sufficient and ungenerous when it refuses to acknowledge that the context it is in extends further than actual urban functions related to guiding anticipated flows of traffic around and through it, creating places for pause and play, with good working conditions, housing and a museum inside, all of which are to profit from one another.

A building is never just a solution to a current task, where it must meet a set of challenges, however complicated. It has an extension in time far beyond these and must be capable of adaptation to other functions when the current one ceases to be relevant. In this light the most important thing is perhaps not to optimize a building for all the things it has to do here and now but to open it up for all one does not yet know will come.

It is impossible to predict what the future will bring, so architecture must therefore work towards a more open programming. Mixing programmes and making architecture more complex is a strategy that OMA has advocated, in which buildings like Blox, by combining several functions, achieve synergetic effects they would not have had if they were separated. But this strategy does not avoid the disadvantages of the Functionalist way of thinking, in which the architecture is formed and built to optimize specific functions. It must be able to survive functional changes; it must have qualities that endure irrespective of the use made of the building.

The use of public space has changed drastically over the past twenty years. A few years ago it was everywhere about motion and exercise. Now growing food in urban gardens is the new black. And before the summer of 2016 no one went around in public spaces catching digital monsters with their telephones. All at once 'Pokemon Go' changed the relationship between the users and public space when it suddenly became the scenery for a worldwide digital game.

Such reinterpretations of the physical spaces, what we expect of them and how we use them are things architecture cannot keep up with. Architecture is an unusually slow art; often five to ten years pass from the planning of a project to its inauguration, and in that period expectations of what it must do can change several times. If architecture is to continue to make sense in such a mutable world, it must have qualities beyond the purely functional.

Lundgaard & Tranberg's architecture points forward to an open programming in which unforeseen changes are already allowed for as a given condition. In this thinking architecture is twisted loose to some extent from the iron grip of functionality. There is something that is more important. Of course there is no point building without living up to all the quantifiable requirements of current knowledge. But it does not become architecture unless it is first and foremost permeated by an artistic feeling for grasping something that is bigger than function, which can be incorporated in the part and the whole and makes it all vibrate.

The eye, the body and the community

The strength of phenomenology lies in the fact that it sees the world as always connected through a body that is in a place. In its perspective there are no abstract spaces or generic cities. All attempts to create this in modernistic housing construction or airports have led to spaces with a thin atmosphere and a palpable deficit of human qualities. We are not freely floating consciousnesses but bodies that are so connected with the world that we cannot distinguish our concepts and thoughts about the world from our ways of being in it.

Philosophically, phenomenology is an attempt to overcome the fragmentation that arose in modern Western thinking with René Descartes's epistemological idea that subject and object were separate. This cast human consciousness out beyond the world. Existentially, phenomenology is an attempt to think the modern individual back into the world. And architecturally, phenomenology is an attempt to create buildings where, by means of an aesthetic fullness, an enrichment of the senses based on an awareness of the character of the place can once more make the body feel at home.

Common to the various aspects of phenomenology is a fundamental experience of fragmentation, where there is a preceding loss that must be healed, and the healing process, if it is possible, goes through showing the individual a way back into the world.

Phenomenological architecture's attention to the close senses of the body is based on the experience of a loss of directly meaningful connectedness with the surroundings in modern culture. The search for sensation in the materials and the experience of atmosphere expresses a longing to reinstate this lost connectedness.

In 'The Eyes of the Skin' Juhani Pallasmaa sets phenomenology against the visual culture he believes has reduced architecture to a question of stimulating the eye, simply of getting a building to look good in a picture. With an assertion by Heidegger that 'the crucial event in modern times is the conquest of the world as image,' Pallasmaa takes up what he sees as a narcissistic and nihilistic tendency in architecture: 'The despotic eye attempts to dominate all areas of artistic production, and this apparently weakens our capacity for empathy, sympathy and participation in the world. The narcissistic eye sees architecture only as a means of expressing oneself and as an intellectual-artistic game entirely without the important mental and social linkage, while the nihilistic eye adds to sensory and mental distancing and alienation.' And he continues: 'The world becomes a hedonistic but meaningless visual journey.'

It is this very distance from the sensory which according to the phenomenologists installs all this unfeeling folly.

It is not hard to find confirmatory examples where nihilism has grown out of visual culture, all the way from the mistreatment of prisoners in Abu Ghraib to the distribution of child pornography in secret networks. But it is not difficult either to find examples of the opposite, where photojournalism has brought empathy and human understanding with it, all the way from the picture of the naked nine-year-old Kim Phuc, who ran screaming with her brothers from their napalm-burnt village, or pictures of the victims of famine in Ethiopia. On social media every day, pictures bring separated people together again but are equally used to pillory and bully people. Image technology is not in itself evil, and even phenomenologically minded architects try to have their built atmosphere captured by cameras and distributed as documentation of their work.

The culture of the image is a condition of life, and its non-tactile nature and references to other places sneak a loss of presence into what fills out our attention span, but by contrast it also helps to create a global consciousness and conscience. Images, like words, are signs used in communication among human beings. It is not the medium but what we say with it that is crucial.

I believe, in other words, that neither the eye nor the culture of the image are the monsters in modern times that Heidegger and Pallasmaa make them out to be. What has, however, radically changed our attitude to being human is access to almost infinite machine power. It is our ability to change our physical surroundings in no time at all that diminishes the value of our own body and senses. We can move over great distances speedily; in the course of just a few years we build enormous projects and new towns where the scale and the execution refer to economics and statistics rather than to us as individual human beings, our senses and our history.

It is not the image but the possibility of moving and manipulating very large bodies of material very quickly that has created a post-human society where all that a single human being can create with the strength of the individual seems in vain if not actually ridiculous. This is why it affects us when we encounter architecture of a particular sensuousness, as it makes us experience that what the body feels is not a matter of indifference. We feel that someone with access to the great forces of construction has thought about us. That is the message and the strength that are built into phenomenological architecture.

But we can also turn phenomenological criticism back against its source and say that phenomenology, in its preoccupation with the loss of presence, overlooks the fact that mankind is perhaps not first and foremost a sensing but perhaps equally a social being.

Ever since Edmund Husserl, from the beginning of phenomenology, there has been a mode of thinking that attempts to heal the rift between subject and object that Descartes had installed in Western thinking. The movement in all phenomenological thinking is the same: we have fundamentally distanced ourselves from the world, and our primary concern is to regain it – also in phenomenological architecture.

From an existential-phenomenological point of view we are aliens in a late modern systemic world. This is a position that assumes that the human being is first a bodily and then a social being. In existential philosophy it has always been difficult to arrive at ethics, because it takes its point of departure in the individual and the feeling of anxiety and isolation. For Kierkegaard the link with God goes through the individual. Heidegger said that existence was being thrown into the world as if there is nothing around us. And Levinas must go by way of the experience of the face of the other as a phenomenon to link all this isolation with an ethical dimension.

But the question is whether phenomenology does not place too much emphasis on the individual's sensing of the world. After all from birth we are linked with one another as social, sign-bearing beings, and perhaps the individual experience of the world is in reality secondary to what we do, experience and communicate in the collective.

The point here is that it is not the leather-wound handrail, the rotary-cut veneer or the hand-made bricks that in the final analysis make the works of Lundgaard & Tranberg Arkitekter that I have described here stand out. It is the way these sensuously meaning-charged materials are used to unite people and form a setting for their relations.

It is more important to create architecture that links us together than architecture that links us with the world. Buildings create distinctions between inside and outside, up and down, and this informs our way of perceiving ourselves and our place in the world. Buildings support the ranking of human beings; you can either be at the top or down in the basement. And they set the boundaries between those who are in and those who are out.

The ability to move freely through a space is the most important thing architecture can give us. We see this in the aula of The Wedge, where students gather and see one another, in Axel Towers with the raised city garden, and in the Playhouse and Kvæsthusbroen's widely different ways of making a broad palette of platforms available for human meetings and gatherings. Care for the surroundings with all the sensuously selected and matched juxtapositions and assemblies of materials involves an aesthetic strengthening of the individual. This increases one's bodily well-being, but it gains its greatest value by being a means of strengthening the community.

The quality experienced is a feeling in the individual that strengthens the atmosphere among those who are present but is experienced as an atmosphere of generosity attributable to the architecture.

Literature

Books:

Stig L Anderson: *Empowerment of Aesthetics*. Wunderbuch 2014

Holger Bisgaard: *Københavns genrejsning 1990-2010*. Bogværket 2010

Martin Heidegger: *Kunstværkets oprindelse*. Transl. from 'Der Ursprung des Kunstwerks'. Samlerens 1994

Martin Heidegger: *Holzwege*. Vittorio Klosterman 1994

Hans-Georg Gadamer: *Sandhed og metode*. Systime 2004

Martin Jay: *Downcast Eyes. The denigration of vision in twentieth-century French thought*. University of California Press 1993

Boris Brorman Jensen and Kristoffer Lindhart Weiss (eds.): *Art of Many – The Right to Space*. Arkitektens Forlag 2016

George Lakoff & Mark Johnson: *Metaphors We Live By*. The University of Chicago Press 1980

Svend Aage Madsen: *Af sporet er du kommet*. Gyldendal 1984

Rowan Moore: *Why We Build*. Picador 2012

Juhani Pallasmaa: *Arkitekturen og sanserne*. Arkitektens Forlag 2014

Maurice Merleau-Ponty: *L'Oeil et l'Esprit*. Gallimard 1964

Synne Rifbjerg: *Hvad tænker arkitekten på?* Arkitektens Forlag 2015

Jørn Utzon: *Arkitekturens væsen. Logbog*. Vol. 1. Edition Bløndal 2004

Vitruvius: *Om Arkitektur*. Ed. Jacob Isager. Syddansk Universitetsforlag 2016

Richard Weston et al.: *Tietgen Dormitory an Imaginary Journey*. Edition Bløndal 2012

Peter Zumthor: *Atmospheres. Architectural Environments – Surrounding Objects*. Birkhäuser GmbH 2006

Periodicals:

Horsens Kraftvarmeværk. Arkitektur DK 5-6 1993

Faaborg Kraftvarmeværk. Arkitektur DK 3 1997

Svendborg Kraftvarmeværk. Arkitektur DK 3 2000

Charlottehaven. Arkitektur DK 3 2002

Christoffer Harlang: CBS Kilen. Arkitektur DK 8 2006

Mari Hvattum: Stedets tyranni, Arkitekten vol 112. 2 2010

Kjeld Vindum: SEB Arkitektur DK 06 2011

Websites:

arkitekturbilleder.dk

axeltowers.dk

ltarkitekter.dk

sorokunstmuseum.dk

unep.org

Vibrations
A Portrait of Houses Designed by
Lundgaard & Tranberg Architects
Translated from the Danish from 'Vibrationer. Et portræt
af huse tegnet af Lundgaard & Tranberg Arkitekter'

Texts © 2016: Karsten R.S. Ifversen;
© 2016 for the reproduced photos: Jens Markus Lindhe
The Danish original edition was published by Strandberg
Publishing A/S
English edition © 2017 Hatje Cantz
This translation of 'Vibrations' is published by Hatje Cantz by
arrangement with Strandberg Publishing A/S.

Translations: James Manley
Copyediting: Wendy Brouwer
Graphic design: Søren Damstedt, Trefold
Typesetting: Trefold
Typeface: Sentinel
Reproductions: Narayana Press, Gylling
Printing: Narayana Press, Gylling
Paper: 140 gsm Prolibro Book Paper
Binding: Buchbinderei Büge, Celle

Published by
Hatje Cantz Verlag GmbH
Mommsenstraße 27
10629 Berlin
Tel. +49 30 3464678-00
Fax +49 30 3464678-29
www.hatjecantz.de
A Ganske Publishing Group Company

Hatje Cantz books are available internationally at selected
bookstores. For more information about our distribution
partners, please visit our website at www.hatjecantz.com.

ISBN 978-3-7757-4357-0
Printed in Denmark 2017

Cover illustration: Playhouse of the Royal Danish Theatre,
Copenhagen. © Photo Jens Markus Lindhe 2017

Frontispiece: Playhouse of the Royal Danish Theatre,
Copenhagen. © Photo Jens Markus Lindhe 2017